STAND UP
STRAIGHT

STAND UP
STRAIGHT

MAJOR GENERAL PAUL NANSON

CENTURY

7 9 10 8 6

Century
20 Vauxhall Bridge Road
London SW1V 2SA

Century is part of the Penguin Random House group of companies
whose addresses can be found at global.penguinrandomhouse.com.

Penguin
Random House
UK

First published in the United Kingdom by Century in 2019

www.penguin.co.uk

A CIP catalogue record for this book is available from the British Library.

Hardback ISBN 9781529124811
Ebook ISBN 9781473576858
Audiobook ISBN 9781473577794

Typeset in 13.5/17pt Vendetta by Jouve (UK), Milton Keynes

Printed and bound in Great Britain by Clays Ltd, Elcograf S.p.A.

Penguin Random House is committed to a sustainable future
for our business, our readers and our planet. This book is made from
Forest Stewardship Council® certified paper.

ABOUT THE ACADEMY

The Royal Military Academy Sandhurst (RMAS) is the place where all officers in the British Army are trained to take on the responsibility of leading their fellow soldiers. During training, all officer cadets learn to live by the Academy's motto: 'Serve to Lead'. Officers who have graduated from Sandhurst include: Sir Antony Beevor, James Blunt, Sir Winston Churchill, Sir Michael Morpurgo, astronaut Tim Peake CMG, Heather Stanning, Nicola Wetherill, Prince William, Duke of Cambridge and Prince Harry, Duke of Sussex. Other nations choose to send their personnel to Sandhurst for officer training because it is recognised as a world-leading military training academy.

ABOUT THE AUTHOR

Paul Nanson is a British Army officer who serves as Commandant of the Royal Military Academy Sandhurst and General Officer Commanding Recruiting and Initial Training Command. During more than thirty years in the British Army, he has served in The Troubles, the Gulf War, the Bosnian War, the Iraq War, and the war in Afghanistan, which saw him appointed a Commander of the Order of the British Empire (CBE) for distinguished services. In his tenure at Sandhurst, he has established the Centre for Army Leadership, one of the world's premier centres for army military leadership.

To all the soldiers who we, as officers, are privileged to serve.

CONTENTS

STAND UP
STRAIGHT

INTRODUCTION

Welcome Address

I look at my watch for the fifteenth time in as many minutes. Still one hour and a half to go . . . The flashes in the distance show where our artillery is hard at work preparing for the upcoming attack. They illuminate the vehicles either side of my own, Scimitar and Spartan reconnaissance tanks waiting patiently for the order to advance. We are in 'Forming Up Place Green' on the border between Saudi Arabia and Iraq. It's February 1991, and I am in charge of a platoon of twenty-four men.

Forming Up Place (FUP) Green marks for us the beginning of the ground offensive stage of Operation Granby, more commonly known by its US title, Desert Storm, the operation to liberate Kuwait. The journey to the FUP has involved weeks of preparation and training. A long and complicated move from our base in Germany, through staging posts in the Saudi desert, to training areas and finally through the American forces who had carved a way through the enemy's minefields for us. The FUP marks the place from which we will launch our advance towards our first objective, 'Brass', an Iraqi artillery position. My platoon is the reconnaissance platoon, tasked with leading the battlegroup – comprised of various units from our own battalion and other regiments – and finding the enemy's positions.

Another look at my watch and still an hour to go. Time to think as I listen to the chatter of the two soldiers who share my tank. Time to think and time to fear. Fear of the unknown, of the unexpected, and fear of failure. What happens if I am the one who, when the time comes, lets the rest down? What if I fail as a leader? This is the first time any of the platoon has been in combat and I am their 25-year-old leader. Leadership has suddenly become very real; a poor judgement or a wrong decision from me and my men might die.

The radio suddenly comes alive and Lance Corporal Bruton looks across at me and says, 'Time to go, boss.' I give the order to advance on the platoon radio and, as twelve tanks start to move slowly out into the desert, the fear fades away and is replaced with a quiet confidence, born of belief in those men around me, in those who lead me and in my own capability. I won't fail because I have been trained by the best – and at the best leadership academy in the world.

THE ROYAL MILITARY ACADEMY

Camberley is a long way from the Iraqi desert. It's actually quite easy to miss the Academy as you drive down the A30 through the town centre. The only give-away is the stone gatehouse set back from the road. Once through it, you are into acres of parkland and lakes, dominated by a series of stately buildings, the grandest of which is Old College with its iconic pillars and parade square.

The Royal Military Academy Sandhurst (RMAS) came into being because British Army officers were failing. Prior to the nineteenth century, if you had the requisite money, the connections or the right background, you could simply buy rank, and command and lead men. One very far-sighted officer, General Le Marchant, decided the British Army needed to properly train and educate young men to lead, so he built the RMAS. Sadly, he never saw it opened – he was killed in the battle of Salamanca – but since 1812, Sandhurst has been developing world-class leaders, and to this day possesses something of a mystique around the world. It's often asked how we create such fine leaders out of young women and men, some as young as nineteen years old, so that they are capable of making difficult and mature decisions in some of life's most demanding environments.

By the time officer cadets complete their training, and graduate or 'pass out' by marching up those famous Old College steps, they have attained a confidence that radiates from their very being. A sense of quiet self-belief that they could be airdropped anywhere in the world and they would quickly learn what was happening on the ground, problem-solve, make informed decisions, and deal with almost any situation thrown at them.

Our graduates have gone on to be world leaders in a whole host of fields, but they all share an affinity – their world-class Sandhurst training. Notable British Sandhurst alumni include: Sir Antony Beevor, James Blunt, Sir Winston Churchill, Sir Michael Morpurgo, Tim Peake CMG, Heather Stanning, Nicola Wetherill, Prince William, Duke of Cambridge, and Prince Harry, Duke of Sussex. The creator of James Bond, author Ian Fleming, also attended but did not complete his Commissioning Course.

So what, you might be asking yourself, is the purpose of this book? Well, an editor at Penguin Random House kindly approached me and asked if I would be interested in writing about the key leadership principles and life lessons from one of the world's top military academies, which might be transferable to everyday civilian life. My immediate thought was *yes*. For a start, it would give me the chance to dispel a few myths about the Academy, but also share some thoughts on what good leadership can look like. For those of you reading this who feel you are not yet leaders, I hope the tips and lessons within these pages will inspire you to cultivate the best of yourself as you go forward.

STAND UP STRAIGHT

What does it mean to 'Stand Up Straight'? For me, the phrase covers a number of themes. Taken literally, it's about making yourself taller, owning your space, putting your shoulders back, and stretching your spine so that you become the optimum size you were designed to be. But it's also about being the fullest and best version of yourself, and holding yourself to a higher standard: to be upstanding and deserving of respect; to be straightforward and honest with others; to be prepared to stand up and step up by being courageous when everyone else is hanging back. After all, we are not just how we present ourselves to the world, but how we act in it, so don't be afraid to make a stand when the moment calls for it. You can take pride and comfort in the fact that, when presented with a choice between making a difference and doing nothing, you were prepared and felt empowered to stand up straight, step up to the plate, and do the right thing – and not just be a bystander. This is part of the bedrock of what we teach at Sandhurst, and what I want to impart to you over the next ten chapters. Be the fullest and best version of yourself – do not waste a single vertebra.

When you stand up straight, you immediately feel stronger and more imposing than when your posture is slumped and your shoulders are hunched, and you will seem stronger to others, too. When someone stands to their full extent and looks you in the eye, it makes you feel as if they are poised and ready for action – it also shows that they have respect for themselves and regard for the person they're addressing. Presence is a strange and intangible force that causes us to look up and pay attention to certain people when they enter a room. It's about the way we hold ourselves physically in a space, and the message it is giving out to others. Being authentic and true to who we are, married with the way we hold ourselves, is key to cultivating a positive presence – and nothing gives a worse impression than a soldier slouching on parade.

Recent discoveries by social scientists have proven that 'power poses' (think of your classic superhero pose: hands on hips, feet a shoulder's width apart, back straight) not only have a huge effect on how others first perceive you, but can entirely change your own behaviour for the better. By striking the right posture, you help recalibrate yourself as you send signals to your brain that can alter your reaction to the situation you're in. These signals encourage your body to produce more testosterone, which makes you feel more confident, and reduce the amount of cortisol, the stress chemical, which makes you feel anxious and prone to unconsciously making yourself smaller.

Social psychologist Amy Cuddy, in her book, *Presence*, details an experiment where she instructed one group of students to hold a 'small' posture, like being slouched over a mobile phone, or slump-shouldered and sitting down, while another held power poses like the one mentioned, or sitting with legs planted wide and arms held up open-palmed in a victory pose. Both groups held these positions for just two minutes and were then given mock job interviews by interviewers who had no idea what they'd just been doing. Without exception, those who had held positive poses came across as more proactive, energised, open and trustworthy, while the slouched students transmitted weakness, ambiguity and a lack of transparency bordering on being untrustworthy.

FORTY-FOUR TESTING WEEKS

When I say 'Sandhurst', how many of you, I wonder, are already imagining a cohort of ruddy-faced public school boys arriving in Jaguars and Land Rovers? Contrary to popular belief, we are not the equivalent of an upper-class meat-factory, churning out clones wrapped in tweed and baronial entitlement.

Our officer cadets, men and women, arrive from a range of religious and ethnic backgrounds; they identify as straight, gay, bisexual; they come from poverty, or from wealth and privilege – sometimes even from royalty; some are spoilt, others have had to learn to fend for themselves. As the new officer cadets gather for the Commandant's Address, sitting in the sanctified cool of the Royal Memorial Chapel, they are surrounded by the engraved names of officers who gave their lives in the First World War, the cap badges of every regiment carved into the ends of the pews, and the names of the officers who perished in the Second World War, never forgotten, in the Book of Remembrance beneath the altar.

In my welcoming address, I tell them that I admire each and every one of them:

> *You are all good enough to be here at the finest military academy in the world. Those of you who are British have all*

been to the Army Officer Selection Board, without doubt the toughest interview in the country, and you got through its physical and mental demands. Those of you from other countries have been hand-picked. You are now here. I won't say it's going to be easy from here on but you've made a significant step. From this moment, I encourage all of you to back yourself. We've seen something in you, and you've all got the potential to march up those steps in forty-four weeks' time as commissioned British and International army officers. It's less about privilege now and all about potential!

SHAPING FUTURE LEADERS

I began my military career in the Territorial Army while still a schoolboy in Lancashire in the north of England, but my regular army career started in January 1986 when I arrived at Sandhurst to start my Commissioning Course to become an officer. For me personally, I owe the Academy a great deal. It set me up for my military career and has, I believe, helped me cope with many of life's challenges. To return as Commandant, years later, was a huge privilege. During my tenure here, I've also been responsible, as Director, for the development of leadership across the wider army.

I believe today's leaders need to be much more aware of themselves and the people they lead. The nature of our adversary has changed. Now they are often un-uniformed and function as a disparate force. Cyber warfare attempts to breach our military infrastructure through the back door of our computers, and we no longer know the face of our enemy. It has become more of a challenge than ever before to shape an officer cadet in readiness for 21st-century warfare and diplomacy. But, despite all this, our core values have not changed and the nature of good leadership endures. Values form the bedrock of how we operate at Sandhurst, and indeed in the army, and whatever the challenges that lie ahead may be, courage, discipline, respect for others, integrity, loyalty and selfless commitment will never become obsolete. You need to be a good person to be a good officer.

Communicating with those around you with integrity and transparency creates trust, and getting to know what makes others tick is vital. Getting to know yourself is equally important, and this is something we're very keen on at Sandhurst: being authentic and not pretending to be something you're not. RMAS brings out a cadet's strengths and weaknesses every day through clear feedback from their fellow cadets and from their instructors, so they know exactly what they need to work on. People have to know they are heading in the right direction and it is a leader's job to convince them they are up to it. There is nothing we will ask them to do that we don't think they're fully capable of succeeding in.

During forty-four testing weeks, we identify and unlock the potential of our officer cadets while breaking the invisible limits cadets have previously imposed upon themselves, building upon the raw materials of their character, heart and integrity by fostering self-discipline and emotional awareness, and soldiering and leadership skills. They will strive for excellence, but they will also be taught not to rest on their laurels.

The majority of these fine young people *will* succeed in securing a commission. They will 'pass out' on the Sovereign's Parade and symbolically enter through the cream-white Corinthian pillars and grand entrance of Old College and into the life of a commissioned officer – an officer who, upon leaving, can be tasked with making complex ethical decisions that have life-and-death consequences. An officer that can be entrusted with the care and well-being of thirty conflict-seasoned soldiers, all of whom are looking for a leader to inspire them.

But we are getting ahead of ourselves. The first step in their – and our – journey starts with positive habit formation. Ready? Let's crack on.

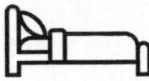

1. THE SANDHURST WAY

The Life-Saving Magic of Tidying Up

The first five weeks at the Royal Military Academy Sandhurst are what our American friends would call a 'boot camp', with an emphasis on intensive drill, fitness training and learning the importance of self-presentation. We don't mind what habits you bring into the Academy, the first five weeks are about teaching you new habits – and hopefully helping you shake off the bad ones. This all-important early training helps to turn a new cadet from a civilian into an officer. Once the desired new habits have been established, the training moves quickly on to more complex tasks, but our approach remains one of repetition: learning by doing, until it becomes routine. After all, routines and training are what we fall back on in tough times.

One of our instructors at Sandhurst tells a story of when he was in Afghanistan and an enemy sniper in a nearby belt of trees was stopping his unit from leaving their camp: 'I squeezed off three rounds in the direction of the sniper, and then moved a few feet to my left, as was my habit. A second later, an AK-47's bullet hissed past me. The Taliban had seen the flash from my muzzle, giving away my position, and had re-sighted their weapons on it. Without this simple, seemingly unremarkable habit – one that had been drummed into me at Sandhurst with such repetition – I would have been dead without question.'

SWEAT THE SMALL STUFF

But it is not just about habit forming. In the first five weeks, the platoon Colour Sergeant, who wears many hats during the cadets' time at Sandhurst – drill instructor, field skills coach, weapons instructor, mentor, parent and confidant – teaches cadets a specific way to iron their uniforms, shine their shoes, tidy their rooms and present themselves properly. We believe that if you look good, you feel good. It might seem obvious, but it is important from the outset to get this stuff right. At 5.55 a.m., the Colour Sergeant orders the cadets to muster behind a black line painted on the corridor floor that runs past every bedroom, and they begin singing the national anthem promptly at 6 a.m. This is followed by an exacting room inspection.

The Colour Sergeant checks for properly ironed clothing, all folded to the dimensions of an A4 piece of paper, and that the bed is made correctly. Everything must be immaculately ironed, even the duvet cover, and everything must adhere to strictly defined measurements. I'm told there are people out there who are curious about how we make our beds – so here is a simple demonstration:

How to make your bed the Sandhurst way

1. Position your flat sheet so that at least six inches of the sheet hangs over each edge of the mattress, then tightly tuck the bottom edge of the sheet under the mattress, leaving the bottom two corners of the sheet hanging down towards the floor.

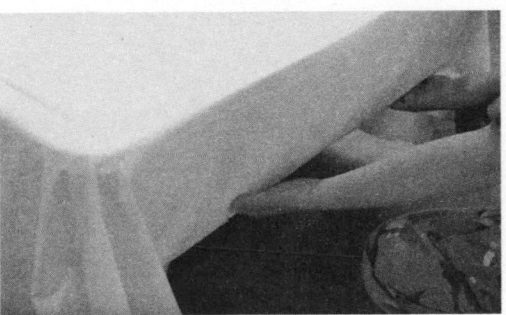

2. To perform a 'hospital corner', pinch your sheet roughly sixteen inches up from the corner and, leading with the pinched portion, cleanly fold up onto the top of the mattress at a 45-degree angle. Keeping hold of your angled fold with one hand, tuck the hanging excess sheet under the mattress.

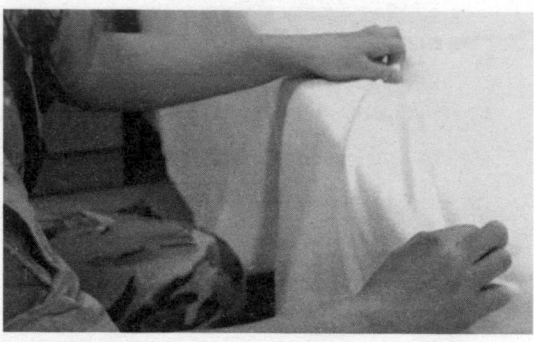

3. Now let your folded section drop down to hang at the side of the bed. Smooth out any wrinkles and, maintaining the crisp fold you created earlier, tuck your new hanging edge under the mattress to secure your hospital corner and repeat this process for the other three corners of the mattress, tucking the top edge

of the sheet under the mattress before tackling the top two corners.

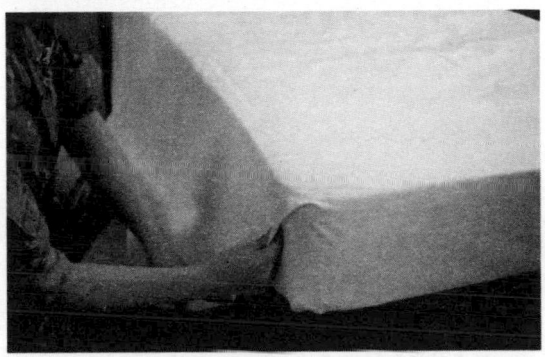

4. Pillows must have excess material tucked in, the closed end, or crease, always facing towards the door.

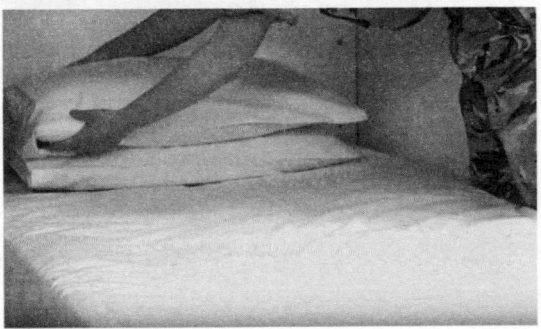

5. To complete your properly made bed, position the duvet so that it only covers the bottom half of the bed. The area of sheet between the duvet and the pillows should be the same length as an A4 piece of paper. Then tuck the duvet tightly under the mattress, starting at the end of the bed, and repeating on both sides.

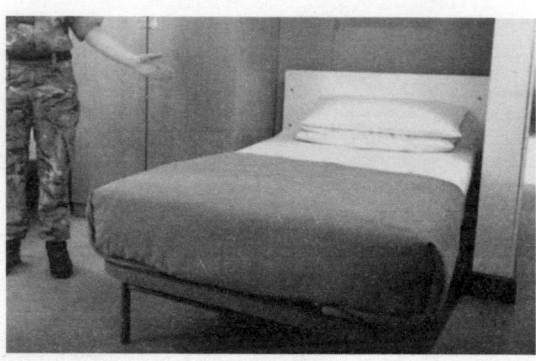

Finally, the Colour Sergeant checks for any traces of dust above the door, on exposed surfaces, or lurking in any nooks or crannies. If the Colour Sergeant identifies any failings, the cadet is faced with a dreaded 're-show' and is given the chance to rectify their failings before another inspection later that same day. These re-shows go on until the cadet passes the inspection. The repetition of action instils these high standards in the cadet and ensures a natural adherence to them in the future. Admittedly, building a new routine at 5.55 a.m. can be a bit of a shock for some.

The reasoning behind these room inspections is to encourage cadets to rapidly develop high standards of discipline and attention to detail, as well as teaching them how to take orders with good grace when they're not feeling at their best. Discipline is one of the British Army's six key values and is built through education, training and practice until it becomes instinctive. Discipline inspires self-control and fosters self-confidence, both of which an officer must possess if they are to lead other men and women. General Rupert Smith once said: 'Discipline is the glue that holds men together when threatened; it is their primary antidote to fear.' The Colour Sergeant is a big part of embedding this level of discipline. Long after the cadets have passed out as fully fledged officers and joined their respective regiments, officers talk of their Colour Sergeant as being like the voice of their conscience, reminding them what to do and when to do it – and believe it or not they won't be shouting in their ear, for that's not the way it's done here any more. At Sandhurst, the Colour Sergeant is an example of the excellent soldiers the cadet will eventually be leading once they have graduated from the Academy. The other piece of the puzzle is the Platoon Commander, who illustrates to the cadets the proper behaviours of an officer and is someone who they can learn from and emulate.

The road to greatness, therefore, starts with a perfectly folded sock. Every Sandhurst graduate will remember every morning having to make our rooms immaculate for inspection. Helmets must sit on the middle of the top shelf, and shirts must hang freely – not bunched together – all facing the same way and with crisply ironed creases in their sleeves. Deodorant, toothbrush and toothpaste must all rest, equidistant from each other, on our wash flannel. Our socks had to be folded in such a way that they looked as if they were grinning back at us. I thought at the time this was all just a pointless way to mess us around. I now understand that, as with everything at Sandhurst, inspections have a practical purpose.

Inspections are about ensuring you can do it for yourself – they impose self-discipline and give a sense of pride. They also ensure we pay attention to the details; that we know what 'good' looks like so we know what standards to set for the people we will eventually lead. If we expect our men and women to be clean and tidy, and to look after their equipment, then we must first learn how to look after ourselves so that we can set the best example. Doing it for yourself needs to become second nature. Only once you have your own house in order can you help the men and women under your leadership to do the same.

When the Colour Sergeant says, 'Well done, you've passed', the cadet feels a sense of achievement as they're rewarded with praise for all the scrubbing, polishing and ironing of collars and cuffs. By starting the day with a small but positive action, they are also unknowingly setting themselves up for further success later that day, because positives breed positives. *At least I've got one thing out of the way and done it properly,* they tell themselves.

Once this sense of pride in everything they do is instilled in cadets, it never leaves them. A Special Forces officer and Sandhurst alumnus told me recently that, even now, he still applies the same level of respect and rigour that he learned to have for his kit to everything he does, whether that be maintaining his bike or writing an email.

PUT YOUR BEST FOOT FORWARD

Drill, or marching in formation, is something we spend much of the first five weeks doing. Although we now use drill primarily for ceremony, it started out as a means of moving soldiers around the battlefield. In days of old, drill would ensure troops formed lines or squares, moved in an orderly fashion from point to point and stood in formation in the face of the enemy. Drill has always been a way of instilling a sense of cohesion and discipline, but I am often asked why we spend so much time doing something we rarely do again as officers once we leave the Academy. The answer is that drill also demands an attention to detail, because if a single person messes up their footwork, salute or shouldering of arms, it radiates a negative effect and throws everyone else off their game, even if everyone else was doing everything right.

During my time at the Academy, there were foot inspections after every arduous exercise. If someone had a blister or athlete's foot, it was immediately sorted out by the medic. At first, I used to wonder, *What's the point of this?* as it all seemed incredibly fussy and overly precious. I was soon to learn that the efficacy of the checks lay in their ability to catch any developing problems before they had an impact on the individual – looking for tell-tale redness and developing sores. The average soldier might be inclined to shrug off these small signs and not take them seriously, especially during a conflict when they might feel that their energy is better spent on other, more obviously 'important' things. However, serious injuries can start as small ones, and if a soldier can't walk or run, they can't fight; if they can't fight they're of no use to their fellow soldiers or commander. Whether you're in 'civilian street' or the army, you need to take care of your people and keep your eyes open to every nuance of how they are operating or feeling.

Well-maintained boots are the first line of defence against the elements, and help soldiers get into the habit of taking care of their feet more generally, too. At Sandhurst, we have a specific way of ensuring our footwear is always at its best, with habitual checks and daily cleaning and upkeep.

How to clean your boots the Sandhurst way

- Before you begin, you will need an 'on' brush and 'off' brush and your polish, and to have removed the laces from your boots.
- Dip your on brush in the polish and spread the polish onto the boot with circular motions. It does not have to be an even application, but make sure you cover every nook and cranny.
- Leave ten to fifteen minutes for the polish to soak into the boots and give them the best shine.
- Using the off brush, using back-and-forth motions and lots of pressure, remove the excess polish from the boots, and bring them to a brilliant shine.

I also remember the endless weapon inspections after exercises, when we had to clean our rifle so assiduously we could almost see our reflection in it and then present it to the Colour Sergeant, who would likely complain about the smallest mite of carbon or smudge of dirt inside the barrel. Again, I thought they were being pedantic. But fast forward four years to the First Gulf War, where I was a Platoon Commander in Iraq with my battalion, the Third Fusiliers, on Operation Granby. We were in the middle of the desert in some of the worst conditions in which to try and keep sand and dirt out of a weapon. We all knew the bottom line was that if our weapons became clogged with sand, they wouldn't operate and neither would we. Weapon inspections were a matter of operational effectiveness, as well as one of individual safety and self-defence. By this stage, keeping my own rifle clean was an ingrained habit, second nature, and a long-established routine born of countless visits to the Colour Sergeant's office so he could check I was doing it right. It was then that I realised why they had put us through so much polishing of brass doorknobs, shining boots and making our bedrooms as clean as an Ikea showroom. Attention to detail was part of Sandhurst's habitual machinery and it would save our lives during conflict.

We are what we turn our attention to. If our first thoughts of the day are that we are worth something or have achieved something worthwhile – especially when others think so too – we will be emboldened to keep on striving. Even if we don't get any form of outward congratulations, we will have the inner satisfaction of knowing we have done something properly, without cutting corners. Think of this first act as a building block towards success.

MAKE YOUR BEST NATURE, SECOND NATURE

I recently read that some 40 per cent of an average person's daily actions are based on habits that happen automatically and unconsciously, as if they are sleepwalking, while the remaining 60 per cent are governed consciously. The brain looks for shortcuts and ways to be lazy, so anything that we repeat on a regular basis soon becomes an assumed habit – whether that's driving a car, going for a run in the morning, playing an instrument or speaking a new language – and the brain then allows itself to relax again.

There is always an opportunity to change your behaviours if you want to. What unhelpful habits would you like to change? Maybe it's losing your temper, opening a bottle of wine the same time every evening, eating too much fried food, hitting 'snooze' and sleeping in, or leaving things to the last minute. All these things are part of learned behaviour. The good news is that you have the ability to shake off unhelpful habits and create positive new ones in their place in a very short space of time. However, if these new actions or traits are to become routine, they demand self-discipline and a keenness of intent – a concerted wish, if you will – to be a better version of yourself. This is what we do at Sandhurst in the first five weeks. We develop potential and bring out the best in our cadets, teach them to identify their strengths and weaknesses, and help them form new and better habits that will help them to be better leaders. It soon becomes second nature for cadets to follow their *best* nature.

Why not have your own 'first five weeks' and seize the moment to have a fresh start and cultivate some new and helpful habits? Ask what it is that you are going to achieve today – possibly even before you go to work – to ensure you have a positive outlook. It might be as simple as tidying your room. The smallest of our actions can have a ripple effect on everything that follows, but this can be so subtle that we might not be able to see it for ourselves straight away. With the benefit of hindsight, we can look back objectively at the end of a day and identify what put us in a bad mood and how things spiralled from there. Conversely, we can also recognise the times when we put our own stamp of positivity on the day, and how that run we took when we could have stayed in bed another half-hour gave us a chance to set ourselves up for that morning's crucial meeting, or gifted us the time to reflect and think through a problem.

Remember, every action begets a *re*action, positive or negative, so always put your best self forward. Take pride in and ownership of your everyday activities. There is nothing wrong with taking a sense of achievement from doing small tasks well. Tune into life's every day details and develop your own self-respect and self-discipline. Check in with yourself to see if what you've done passes muster, maybe even reward yourself if you like what you see and, if you have responsibility for others, make sure you are in good order if you expect them to be. Who knows? This might be an opportunity to realise your own untapped potential.

How could you better start your day? Challenge yourself to form one new helpful habit . . . Whatever you choose to do, it really can't be as bad as standing behind that black line for morning inspections at 5.55 a.m.

2. LONG DAYS, SHORT WEEKS

The Way You Spend Your Day is the Way You Live Your Life

During the Second Gulf War, there was wide-scale looting in Basra after the overthrow of Saddam Hussein. We found ourselves in a power vacuum: there was no longer any local law and order, and so we had to try to impose it as best we could ourselves. When faced with looters, I directed my soldiers that if people were stealing food then it was probably because they were hungry and were trying to help their families survive, whereas if they were stealing possessions from other people's houses then that was a criminal act and we should arrest the offenders. At this stage of the War, there was no remaining official infrastructure in place in Iraq, and consequently there were no police stations, or prisons to put the people we'd arrested in. In light of this, we took the offenders back to our security base – a ramshackle maritime naval building – and told them that they were to be detained for two days and set them to work making our base safer. We tried to explain that the looting they had been doing was wrong and that this labour was meant as a punishment. We made them fill sandbags, help us prepare our defensive positions and create a safer environment. Of course, the troops were also providing food and water to keep them going and, naturally, sharing the occasional cigarette or chocolate bar. After two days, as promised, we let them go. We could do little else.

Then an extraordinary thing happened ... They started to come back, bright and early, over the following mornings. In fact, one morning, there were so many people that they had formed a queue outside the patrol base. They wanted to work with us not only because we were paying them with food, but also because it gave them a much-needed sense of purpose. As one explained, it gave him a sense of self-worth at a time when life had lost its structure.

Seneca, the Roman Stoic philosopher, once said: 'If a man knows not to which port he sails, no wind is favourable.' In other words, without a direction to follow or a purpose to aim for, we drift aimlessly or go round in circles. In the army – whether at war or in peacetime – a soldier's day is governed by specific goals and the corresponding methods through which they will be achieved. These goals give the soldier a sense of meaning, something tangible towards which they direct their energy. Without this structure, a soldier can easily become listless and their time no longer feels like a valuable commodity. Goals give us a sense of purpose and momentum while we strive to achieve them, and we gain self-confidence and self-respect upon their successful completion. It's vital to have goals, and to keep developing ourselves through fresh challenges. Having a purpose is what gets us up in the morning, for when we lose the 'why', the 'what' becomes pointless. We all need a reason to jump out of bed rather than slither out.

THE IMPORTANCE OF 'COMMAND TIME'

We talk a lot about the importance of sleep at Sandhurst. We've worked out that 6.5 hours is the minimum amount of sleep a cadet should have, because not only are they exhausted by their studies and physical training, but also their brains are still fine-tuning in the pre-frontal cortex (the reasoning area). This part of the brain keeps developing up until around the age of twenty-seven, chiefly at night while you're asleep. At Sandhurst our cadets get up early as there is so much that needs to be packed into the forty-four weeks of officer training. In order to avoid burnout, we advise they go to bed between 10 and 10.30 p.m. at the very latest in order to be up at around 5.30 a.m. Believe me, it takes very little persuasion.

As for the rest of us? Well, we need our sleep too. A rested mind is one that can think efficiently and clearly under pressure, and one that can be creative. A good leader is one who is prepared to do everything their soldiers can; however, every leader needs to learn to take time out, 'reflection time', obligatory rest and recovery, so they can gather their energies to make the right decisions for their team. We call it 'Command Time': the taking of much-needed rest – both physically and mentally – to ensure you are functioning well, so you can continue to make the best decisions.

How much sleep are you getting? Do you check in with your-self regularly? If you're going to be at your most effective, you need to learn when to lead and when to rest – and you need adequate sleep to be able to work at your optimum. One of our alumni recently told me a story about a multi-national firm they were consulting, after they'd stepped down from army life. The firm had been seriously rattled by a crisis and was on the brink of going under. The CEO was in fire-fighting mode and, having stayed awake for all-hours in order to hold everything together, he had become frayed at the edges and ineffective. Not good news when he had to talk to the press. The first thing the Sandhurst alumna advised was that the CEO took his Command Time and they politely sent him straight home to bed. Time to sleep, time to think, time to bounce back fighting. After taking the time to restore himself, the CEO was able to come back and deal with the problem in a much more commanding manner than before.

THE EARLY BIRD MAKES BETTER DECISIONS

My Command Time often takes the form of running. While I was a cadet at Sandhurst, I'm not sure I fully appreciated all the early-morning runs – but I certainly do now. Imagine 700 acres of elegant parkland and mature woodland scattered with lakes, sports fields, Georgian architecture and manicured lawns. For me, nothing beats an early run or a visit to the gymnasium to wake myself up and get the synapses flashing in the old grey matter. Exercise sends a message to the brain to release serotonin, the pleasure chemical, as a kind of reward, while the increased circulation of blood improves your alertness and energy. The simple habit of slipping on a pair of trainers and running shorts as soon as I wake up and launching myself into this natural peace and quiet is one I never like to miss. Exercise to me is vital: it tells me I've still got juice in the tank, that I care about my health and respect my body, and that gives me an appetite for the day. It's such an ingrained habit now that if I don't make time for it I feel restless all day. Taking a run, even in bad weather, is a small gift from me to myself. It helps me start my day with a sense of achievement.

One of my runs takes me around the lake, the mist hovering over the water, the early-morning sun flashing through the trees and glittering upon its surface. Sometimes, as I head into the woods, past giant trees – just saplings when Sandhurst's founder, Le Marchant, established the Academy in 1812 – I'll see deer grazing. My best thinking time is when I'm running. The repetitive motion helps me settle my mind and I feel grounded. For me, this Command Time is invaluable, and I'm lucky to have the time and the space at Sandhurst to run most mornings.

People often rush to make decisions and, admittedly, sometimes we are forced to make snap choices or risk missing an opportunity but, where possible, I always try to run before I make an important decision. I am often required to make speeches in front of large numbers of people, and I always like to go for a run to help order my thoughts as I put my words together. Time to think. I often jot down notes on how I am going to tackle the problem, then go for a long run to allow my mind the space to think it through. When I come back, I have often thought of a completely different – and much better – approach to the problem. Where possible, take yourself out of your immediate environment and give yourself time to think.

I asked some of the staff here at Sandhurst about their early-morning habits and their thinking time and their responses didn't come as a surprise. One said: 'My routine is a bike ride or a run in the early morning and then I am ready for the day. It gives me a sense of satisfaction that I've done something for myself, for my own health.' While another said: 'I like to have everything ready to go far in advance. I'll pack my kit up for an exercise a few days before. If you have less things to worry about coming up in the week, you have more time to concentrate on other things. I'm up around 5.30 a.m. most days and cycle to work. I always get my bike ready and work things packed up and ready to go the night before.'

The benefits of getting up early and exercising more than justify leaving the warmth of your bed. Whether it's swimming, meditation, a Pilates routine or simply taking a few stretches to get 'into your body', what counts is that you are prepared to invest time in yourself and put your stamp on the day instead of just drifting through it. That alone makes you feel good about yourself.

SET YOUR CLOCKS TO 'SANDHURST TIME'

For cadets at Sandhurst, mornings typically begin between 5.30 and 6 a.m. and, before the sun has even started to settle upon the ropes in the Montgomery gymnasium and the Barossa assault course, cadets are dressed and ready to go. Their goal is clear: to keep going, one foot in front of the other, until they have fought their way through forty-four tough weeks that will turn them into officers. But to get there, the journey is broken down into a series of challenges that they move through methodically. Please don't take this literally but, as the saying goes, the best way to eat an elephant is in chunks. Set your goal high then break it down into digestible sections, so you can move purposefully toward it, ticking off the stages as you go. Ask any Sandhurst cadet, past or present, to describe life at the Academy and they will talk of 'long days and short weeks' or define time in terms of exercises and tests that act as waypoints that are ticked off on the road to graduation.

'Sandhurst Time' is always five minutes early. It was drilled into me while I was a cadet, so I worry if I am not keeping to that. In fact, many of us who have come through the Academy set our watches five minutes ahead. 'H-hour', in army speak, is the time at which an attack or advance begins, when you cross your line of departure. It has to be precise because other components of the army are supporting you – the artillery, the air support, etc. – and they all work off H-hour. If you go too early, the fire will not have had the necessary 'shock effect' on the enemy; too late, and the fire will have stopped and the enemy will have had time to recover, and you will have wasted the 'shock effect'.

Consequently, it's drilled into us at Sandhurst that the worst thing you can do is to be late. BATUS (British Army Training Unit Suffield) is a place in Winnipeg, Canada where the British Army prepare battlegroups for operations. As a Captain, and second-in-command of the Fusiliers A Company, I spent time at BATUS taking part in armoured warfare manoeuvres. Excitingly, this was the first time the new Warrior armoured fighting vehicle had ever been deployed to Canada. The exercise is designed to allow us to test our equipment, our drills and procedures, and ourselves. It consists of a series of demanding tasks, sometimes using live ammunition, sometimes using a simulated enemy.

On one occasion, we had been there for four weeks and, although the tank showed no signs of flagging, we were tired, incredibly so. We'd been warned that the following morning there was to be a battlegroup attack, which involved two armoured infantry companies and a tank squadron, supported by artillery and engineers. All these moving parts had to coordinate and come together at a specific point in time – H-hour. We would receive radio orders overnight giving us the details, and in particular the when and the where. After checking we had people taking turns on 'stag' – who would stay awake and listen out for the order on the radio – we ensured we had everything ready for the morning and, finally, we slept.

The next morning, I woke up in broad daylight and immediately thought, *We should be moving by now*. I could hear the radio blaring in the back of one of the vehicles and, to my horror, found the radio stag asleep. I could hear the other parts of the battalion already moving into position. I got the Company Commander out of bed and told him what was going on – or rather what wasn't – and that we were going to be late. His face went pale. We couldn't miss H-hour! In a scene reminiscent of a comedy film, we gave the order to 'Move now!' and loaded the armoured vehicles by shoving everything in the back – literally. (I might clarify at this point that *usually* everything gets packed away incredibly neatly, with much of the equipment on the outside of the vehicles and the sensitive parts – our people and our weapons – on the inside.) There were soldiers running around all over the place, and we drove like devils to get to where we needed to be. Everybody knew we absolutely couldn't be late for H-hour, because our absence would have a negative impact on the rest of the battalion, and A Company would be the ones to blame for the failed attack. We made it – just – and I can remember my Company Commander announcing calmly that A Company was in position, as though we had been ready for hours.

Horatio Lord Nelson once said: 'I have always been a quarter of an hour early and it has made a man of me.' At Sandhurst we treat time as a precious commodity and, not surprisingly, punctuality is a given. The more we master our poor time-keeping habits, the more confidence and respect we cultivate for ourselves and from others. Being late shows a lack of discipline and self-control, and is disrespectful to the arrangements and the promises we have made with others. It also makes us feel disorganised, whereas being on time shows we are conscientious and ready for action. Being late is also a form of theft because, while you're taking extra time for yourself, the people who were on time are forced to wait and are robbed of minutes that cannot be claimed back.

MAKE YOUR MOUNTAINS INTO MOLEHILLS

A life lived well is a life well planned, and in order to get somewhere on Sandhurst Time, be it a battalion attack or a staff meeting, we all need to plan a few steps ahead. The same goes for achieving any major goal. Anticipating consequences and planning for all eventualities puts you in a much better place to succeed in your goals. At Sandhurst, we teach cadets about battle planning. Once we fix a mission objective in our crosshairs, we then work out how to get there: considering the possible obstacles ahead and all the things that might go wrong, mapping out possible contingency plans, and thinking through what we might have to do instead if things don't go as predicted. As a recent alumna said, 'Sandhurst taught me to think about the third bend ahead of me, not just the one I'm staring at.' Are you prepared? Do you have everything in place to start your march towards success? Equipped or not, sometimes you just have to get on with it, otherwise you will always find reasons to prevaricate. The way we spend our days is the way we spend our lives, so if you're someone who keeps putting off achieving your goal until a more convenient time, ask yourself: 'Why?' What is it that is holding you back?

Sometimes a goal can seem like too big a mountain to scale,

even just thinking about it. In moments like these, it can help to start viewing the path towards your goal as a series of smaller challenges, achievable milestones on your route to success. Nobody climbs Mount Everest by constantly looking up at that menacing jagged peak. If they did, they'd either make mistakes and fall down a crevasse from not focusing on the ground under their feet, or they'd never leave base camp, overwhelmed by the almighty scale of the task ahead. Seasoned climbers break the ascent into a series of rest camps on their path to the summit. And between these camps, they walk, raising one foot after the other, focusing just a few feet ahead of them. Find a goal worthy of your precious time and energy, and then break it down into waypoints that feel achievable. Identify your path and its potential obstacles, seize each day by its scruff, and keep putting one foot in front of the other to drive through your personal waypoints and achieve your goals.

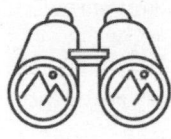

3. TIGHTEN YOUR CHINSTRAP

Get to Know Your Threshold of Failure

It might come as a surprise, but many of our cadets from financially stable, happy and supportive families struggle in their first few weeks at Sandhurst. They arrive with a near-spotless record of triumphs — captaining their First XV rugby team, playing hockey for their county, being chosen as head boy or girl, prefect, monitor etc . . . in short, they are used to being a big fish in a small pond, used to winning and excelling. The upshot is that many have thus far never drunk from the cup of disappointment. They struggle because they have rarely dealt with failure.

Others come from more challenging backgrounds. Some of our cadets have endured poverty or family difficulties; some have even been homeless. They have had to learn to deal with things not turning out as planned and, despite all the obstacles and setbacks, have navigated a way through a variety of problems and prevailed. The first five weeks are designed to bring the cadets up to a common baseline, and it doesn't take long for the more sheltered cadets to catch up. Sandhurst introduces a healthy approach towards failure to all our cadets, flipping it from being something feared into something that is integral to self-development.

As a cadet, I was placed in command of a section during the attack phase of a training exercise. With my Colour Sergeant watching closely, I came under fire from the enemy. The section quickly went to ground and started to return fire. This was my moment to make a decision. I froze. For whatever reason, I couldn't seem to react and I ended up appealing to the Colour Sergeant for help. It was a total failure and I have never forgotten the debrief I received. Since then, whenever I face a difficult decision, I remember that day at Sandhurst and the advice I received: *Right or wrong, make a decision*. It's better to be doing something with momentum than sitting in a ditch like a stationary target.

At no future point in their career will the officer cadets be watched more closely by those around them than during their time at Sandhurst. The vigilance and scrutiny of their platoon staff and their fellow cadets ensure that they work on their development areas with constant feedback to keep them on track, with their peers helping to bring them up to speed for the good of the team.

It's important for all cadets to manage their expectations. One of the painful lessons they experience early on in the course is that they may no longer be the best at something. As life teaches us, there is usually someone better and so, in response to this, we encourage cadets to celebrate the diversity present among their company. All of us have very different strengths, whether it's map reading, obstacle courses, weapon training or academic ability. Cadets learn very quickly to have the humility and self-awareness to admit to their areas of weakness and seek advice from those among their company who are stronger. A good team is symbiotic, and those in need of your help on one day will return the favour the next day when you find the roles are reversed. In southern Africa, they have a saying: *Ubuntu* – 'I am, because we are'. In fact, *Ubuntu* is just part of a longer Zulu phrase: *Umuntu ngumuntu ngabantu*, which literally means that a person is a person through other people, through their community or, at Sandhurst, their team. We become stronger together by fostering teamwork and through the distribution of diverse skills.

TIGHTEN YOUR CHIN-STRAP

Great potential is one thing, but fulfilling it is another. In life, you'll come across star performers who haven't yet tasted failure and it can come as a shock to them when things, as they inevitably do, go wrong. Sir Winston Churchill knew a thing or two about the extremes of failure and success – perhaps learned during his time as an officer cadet at Sandhurst – and wisely said: 'Success is the ability to go from one failure to another with no loss of enthusiasm.' He didn't mean that we should keep constantly failing with enthusiasm, but rather that failure is part of the roots of success. At Sandhurst, we encourage our officer cadets to think their way through failure and ask themselves what else can be done, bringing out their initiative and developing their self-worth and confidence.

During my Commandant's address in the Memorial Chapel at the end of the first week of the first term, I explain to the cadets: 'One of the principles we use here is that we will push you to what we call "the threshold of failure". This is the zone where you will learn most about yourself. We will put you in positions where you will probably fail, and that's OK, because it's here you will learn. As long as you do learn, dust yourself off, tighten your chin-strap and bounce back, then that's a good thing.'

At Sandhurst, we learn how to solve problems and it often takes more than one attempt to get something right. We all have to fail in order to succeed, but we help our cadets to redefine the parameters of failure, and to learn that it is something both forgivable and temporary. In this increasingly complicated world, more so than at any time before, they'll face things they don't have an answer for, the risks will be greater and come at them with more caprice than ever, and part of their resilience training is realising that they will not always be right, and things will not always be successful.

If we want resilient officers, they have to be able to think freely and creatively for themselves and so we ask them questions that stimulate their initiative, constantly unpicking their failures with them, helping them explore what is not working and why, and understanding that getting it wrong is often a necessary step on the path to getting it right. Sure, it's a nice feeling to win all the time, but you can learn so much more from failure. Our approach at Sandhurst is one of positivity, keeping optimistic that there is a way through every challenge to a solution on the other side; we just haven't found it yet. Try to learn to smile through adversity. Failure is a matter of mind-set, and the positive – or negative – ways in which you choose to view it.

FLOAT LIKE A BUTTERFLY, BOUNCE BACK LIKE A SPRING

If we can self-adjust and learn from our mistakes then we are better for it. A boxer does not become a world champion overnight. To get to that crowning moment, they have to learn how to pick themselves up off the canvas when they are beaten and to focus on areas of their craft that are lacking. Maybe their defence is weak and they are taking too many body-shots; each weakness that they identify and correct makes them a better, more complete fighter.

Remember when Muhammad Ali fought the then unbeaten, 25-year-old George Foreman in the historic 1974 fight billed as 'The Rumble in the Jungle'? Foreman was deemed *unbeatable* and had won all but four of his thirty-seven fights by knockouts, but against all odds Ali – the older fighter – came out on top through self-belief and dogged optimism (and maybe a little sorcery). The way you view yourself is vital. If you don't think you can do something, there is no way you can expect your team to believe you can either. You have to have faith in yourself and your ability to do and say the right thing even if, temporarily, others may have lost faith in you. In moments like these, you have to back yourself, because you and you alone are the master of your self-morale.

Fear of failure can be a massive driver for many successful people, and it's staggering how many of us – including myself – use it to propel us through difficult times. For some of us, though, failure can turn into self-sabotage, and at the Academy's School of Leadership, Security and Warfare, we have a forward-thinking unit at the very vanguard of modern psychology, known as the Department of Communication and Applied Behavioural Science, where cadets are taught techniques to build their mental resilience and self-esteem. The unit is run by psychologists and academics, and its aim is to empower future officers with greater emotional awareness of both themselves and their troops. One of our directing staff, Gareth Bloomfield, is an ex-police detective and psychologist who teaches our cadets to view themselves in a positive, optimistic way. Here follows some of the theory behind his teaching:

Psychologist Martin Seligman did some work into what makes an optimist, identifying three key factors:

- How I see myself
- How I perceive my actions affect the future
- Whether I think those changes are meaningful or not

For example, an officer cadet is taught how to do a section attack, a very practical exercise. First they go through the technique in a classroom a week before doing it for real. Then they are the section commander and, inevitably, something goes wrong for whatever reason, mainly because we give them a huge amount of information to absorb in an unrealistically short space of time. We do this on purpose. If they say to themselves, *I'm an idiot, every time I'm given a task like this to lead I screw it up*, we provide an explanation as to why it didn't go as well as it might have done, helping them reframe positively, helping them to tell themselves:

- I'm not an idiot but I'm going to learn from my mistakes.
- Next time, I'm going to make this work.
- Just because I've done this wrong, it doesn't mean it's going to affect the rest of my day.

'Resilience', says Bloomfield, 'comes from the Latin word *resilio*, meaning "to spring back". Whoever we are, we all experience highs and lows, successes and failures. Sometimes we get bent out of shape by the obstacles life throws in our path. When this happens to cadets, we help them understand themselves, teach them how to change their thought patterns and how to put themselves back together again, only stronger. So by making them fail and then unpicking and reviewing that failure with them, it means that, next time it happens, they will know what to do.'

So, back yourself and remember these sage words spoken by General Sir John Hackett: 'They must be able to manage failure as well as success, for failure is seldom final and the person helped on from one failure may well fail no more.'

4. PACK YOUR BERGEN

You Don't Have to be a Minimalist, But it Helps

The more thought you give to what goes in your bag, the better equipped you are for what lies further down the line. If it's raining and you're heading into the Brecon Beacons, you'll need the appropriate clothing. If you are going there for more than two days, then accordingly you'll need more clothes to last you, as well as more food rations. This sounds very basic, but you'd be surprised how many cadets don't give sufficient thought to packing their bags and end up learning their lesson the hard way – after all, they have to carry it.

During the first five weeks we teach cadets how to pack their fighting equipment – Bergens (rucksacks) and belt order (a series of pouches worn on a belt around the waist) – and, perhaps more importantly, *what* to pack. The Colour Sergeant painstakingly lays out all the items that need to be carried, explaining to the cadets why each one is important, before demonstrating how to pack – and then they are tested on it. Before key exercises or tests, there will be a kit inspection (yes, another inspection) to ensure they have all the right equipment. Cadets are required to lay out the items, as per the kit list, for the Colour Sergeant's attention. Woe betide the cadet who misses something – foot powder, spare socks, needle and thread – and woe betide the cadet whose water bottle isn't full or whose toothbrush is too worn. We always pack our bags in the same order. That way we will always know what is in which section and how far down we need to reach for it, and we are better able to find things easily in a hurry, or even in the dark.

THE ABCs OF PACKING

- ### Accessibility

  It's important to pack in reverse order of likely need, prioritising the equipment that you'll need to use regularly – or need quickly – by positioning them near the top of the bag. The army Bergen has two compartments within its lid, an inner and an outer pocket, and it's wise to use these to store things such as your map and compass, your gloves and warm hat, a torch, a waterproof Bergen cover, and a personal first aid kit, for quick and easy access in the event of an emergency or a sudden change in the weather. Following the same logic, it's best to keep your waterproof clothing at the very top of your Bergen's main compartment, storing other things like your ration packs, wash kit and additional warm clothing beneath it. A good tip is to try to store all these different items in their own sealed bag, to ensure they're kept dry because, although we use our Bergens in all manner of climates and weathers, they are definitely not 100% waterproof. At the very bottom of our bags we keep a spare set of uniform – in case we get completely wet-through or badly damage the set we're wearing – and store our sleeping bag. Both of these should also be kept in their own individual dry bags. Believe me, there is nothing worse than having to climb into a soggy sleeping bag at the end of a long day's march.

- **Balance**

  A heavier balanced backpack is easier to carry than a lighter unbalanced backpack. So, now you know the order to pack your kit, it's a good rule of thumb to keep the weight evenly distributed and balanced on both sides. An imbalanced rucksack puts unequal pressure on one side of your body, and you might attempt to compensate for the uneven load by modifying your posture or gait, putting unnecessary extra strain on certain parts of your body. Not ideal when you have a long march ahead of you. If your Bergen is top-heavy, it will be hard to maintain your balance while carrying it, especially when you encounter obstacles or have to navigate sloping terrain. Conversely, a bottom-heavy Bergen will hinder your stride and may sit uncomfortably on your back and hips. The key to a perfectly balanced Bergen is to pack the dense, heavy items like food rations close to the body so that they sit in the mid-level of your pack, somewhere between your shoulder blades and the bottom of your ribcage.

• Compactness

Finally, a compact Bergen is much easier to carry than a loosely packed one and so, when packing your gear, it's important to effectively utilise the space you have available. When packing, look for dead spaces and fill them in with smaller items like socks or ration packs. Some items, such as your dry clothing or sleeping bags, can be compressed down to sometimes half their size with the help of a compression sack. Our Bergens also come with adjustable straps that we can tighten to help further compress our packs into a more compact and manageable load. The more compact you make your bag, the less space there will be for heavier items to shift around and unbalance – and undo – all your careful packing.

Once you learn the trick of packing, it never leaves you. I still find myself packing the same way now, even when I am going on holiday or away for business. I make a list of what I might need, and then lay it all out before checking it off my list as I pack the suitcase. I have also found it useful to check my soldiers' equipment, no matter how experienced they might be. Give a soldier a big Bergen and they will do their best to fill it! Ensuring your soldiers are carrying only what is required for the mission is one of many leadership tasks. If they're carrying too much, they will become fatigued too quickly; too little and the phrase is 'travel light, freeze at night!'. The trick is to pack precisely what you need.

Battlefield discipline demands we live by certain rules when out in the field. Equipment is taken out of a rucksack, used, and then immediately packed up again. Our kit is always neatly stored away for next use, and ready to grab and run with if we need to move out quickly or head to safety if things go wrong. A soldier on a wet winter exercise will pack the things they need to keep warm, dry and watered at the top of their bag for easy access. Likewise, they will keep their night gear in a dry bag deep in their Bergen and, at the end of the day, the soldier will peel off the wet clothes and climb into the dry ones so they can keep as warm and as comfortable as possible, and can get a good night's sleep – and *that* is definitely something that is great for the morale. Discipline comes in the morning, when you then have to repack your warm, dry clothes and put your wet ones back on!

THE SEVEN QUESTIONS

Everything we do at Sandhurst focuses on being as prepared as possible for whatever may happen. Preparation for anything important to you in life is vital, be it doing research before a holiday to an exotic destination – checking what injections are required, the safety of the country – or executing a company takeover and doing your due diligence thoroughly beforehand.

The Sovereign's Banner is awarded at the end of each year to the platoon which has won the most physical and educational challenges. One such winning team included a cadet who had excelled himself as a leader in the 'log race' — a gruelling test of strength and endurance whereby teams race around the grounds of the Academy carrying a tree trunk. The team leader thought ahead by running the route himself with a GoPro camera, and giving a PowerPoint presentation to his team the evening before the race, identifying all the difficult change points that might slow them down. Because they knew the ground and the stops, they won. Simple preparation on the part of the leader meant that he did not find himself under the same level of pressure as the other team leaders, who were less prepared. If you prepare properly, you can master anything.

One way we're taught to analyse a proposed course of action at Sandhurst is by using a technique known as 'The Seven Questions':

The Seven Questions

1. What is the situation and how does it affect me?
2. What have I been told to do and why?
3. What effects do I want to have, and what direction must I give?

> 4. Where and how can I best accomplish each action or effect?
>
> 5. What resources do I need to accomplish each action or effect?
>
> 6. When and where do these actions take place relative to each other?
>
> 7. What control measures do I need?

The Seven Questions exercise, or 'Combat Estimate' as it is sometimes called, is used to provide a logical handrail to aid better decision making. It's not intended to be a simple checklist process; instead the questions are crafted to encourage a fundamental understanding of a situation. Plans made using this method will be flexible and agile, able to be adjusted in the moment. Although we primarily use the Seven Questions when planning an attack, their versatility means that you could use them to help plan another kind of big event, even a wedding.

When planning an attack, we use the questions to consider a variety of factors and plan for them accordingly: where the enemy is located; whether the desired route is clear; what the ground conditions are like; whether there will be an impact on the local population. The same principles can be applied to your wedding preparations, too: considering whether it is likely to rain (investigate cover options, like marquees) or be unusually cold (consider renting additional heating sources); whether there are any dietary requirements that need to be catered for; whether everything is accessible for elderly relatives or disabled guests and, if not, what measures might be taken to accommodate them (wheelchair ramps, reserving a seat for them close to the front if they're hard of hearing) . . . and so on and so forth.

At the end of the Seven Questions exercise, we have developed a plan, considering several different options and winnowing them down before selecting the best course. By applying this planning process, we develop a detailed understanding of an event and its potential problems while also identifying possible solutions and providing ourselves with the flexibility to adapt to changing circumstances. For instance, if there is unusually bad traffic along the proposed bridal route to the ceremony, it is far better to have already identified alternative routes that are suitable for the bridal car ahead of the big day, instead of frantically trying to search for one when you are under pressure and at risk of running late. This can help you focus on staying calm, enjoying the moment, and achieving the overall goal of the wedding.

Think about the things that are important to you, goals that you have set yourself. What is getting in the way of them? Can you strip them back, and simplify them to make them more achievable? What is your MO; your mission objective? For example, if you want to improve your fitness, ask yourself the tough questions: what's your diet like, how much sleep are you getting, are you exercising sufficiently? The more honest you are with yourself, the easier it is to reach your target. Looking beyond your more concrete goals, the same can be said of staying in a toxic relationship, or tolerating a role at work you're not happy with. It's important to prioritise. If being happy is key to you, then start identifying and unpacking the unnecessary elements in your life and replacing them with more helpful, positive ones. Try putting it down on paper, and ask yourself, 'What do I need?' and 'What do I need to lose?'

THINKING OUTSIDE THE BERGEN

The way in which we pack our Bergen can be used as an analogy for the way we live our life. While the way we fill our rucksack at

Sandhurst has a physical impact, the way we choose to pack our lives – and the metaphorical burdens we carry around with us – can have an effect on us too; particularly on our mental health. By taking a little more time to take stock of the way we pack our day we can get so much more done and avoid squandering precious hours. It sounds simple and it is, but it works. We can make our life easier by assessing the usefulness of that which we are carrying, be it physically or emotionally, and if it doesn't serve our purpose then we should jettison it. The more you get your house in order, the easier and less hectic life becomes. Some things in life will be good for you, while others can drain you and are the equivalent of a dead weight in your Bergen.

During the First Gulf War, our battalion was involved in a significant incident in which many lives were lost from a single platoon. An individual within the platoon was injured and, in those days, if you were wounded you were sent back home. In time, he physically recovered and returned to his regiment; however, he never really got better within himself. This was because he'd never had a chance to talk about what had happened with us: his fellow soldiers who had fought with him, and who understood exactly what he'd been through. Unlike this individual, we were still out there together for months after the incident, and that meant that we were able to deal with and process the violence and loss of life we had seen because we could talk about it as a group and heal naturally. There's something very cathartic about not keeping things inside, and talking them through with your friends. During the War we had a ritual where a group of us came together in the evening to cook our track rations and shoot the breeze. It was something we looked forward to, and it was amazing the variety of things we talked about: our wives at home, kids, fears and worries . . . all over a helping of baked beans under the stars. For us, food was a kind of enabler to those deeper conversations, and those precious meals allowed us to offload and start healing ourselves internally.

At RMAS there's a popular trick cadets play on each other before field exercises: secretly slipping something weighty, usually their iron, into someone else's Bergen to see if they will clock it. And while we fully encourage the use of irons in Old College barracks, they are pretty useless in the field. How many irons do you have in your emotional Bergen? If you feel you may be holding on to unnecessary burdens, ask yourself: *Do I really need to keep carrying them?* At Sandhurst, cadets are actively encouraged to get things off their chests. It's important to talk about any worries that you feel might be weighing you down and sapping your precious mental energy. It might feel tricky to open up at first and let others in, but a problem shared is a problem halved. Share the load – you don't have to struggle on alone.

5. BELIEVE IN SOMETHING BIGGER

Learn to Harness the Power of Your Team

Wolves, we've known for some time now, are highly socialised animals which thrive on collaboration, companionship, strict discipline and an established hierarchy. But it may also surprise you to discover that they are also remarkably compassionate towards one another. The weakest *beta* (follower) will never be left at the back of the pack to lag behind and get lost; it will always be insulated in the middle of the group, with an *alpha* (leader) at the front, and another *alpha* (often the leading alpha's mate) at the rear.

Cadets at Sandhurst are told from day one to establish their strengths and weaknesses as a platoon, for each individual brings their own skills to the table. Just like a wolf pack, what gets the cadets through Sandhurst's 44-week course is teamwork, and supporting each other in finessing individual areas of weakness in order to make everyone stronger as a whole. Alpha wolves lead from the front and by example. They make the call on whether or not an approaching bear is worth tackling for food, or whether the risks are too high to swim across a fast-flowing river to the other side. And a good leader is a strong, inspiring one whose success is measured in the health and happiness of its pack. If the pack is struggling, another wolf will challenge the alpha for its position. Wolves don't just survive but flourish through teamwork, constant communication, knowing their place and role within the pack and respecting their leaders. Maybe there is something we can learn from them.

The British Army is made up of teams within teams and, within each of these teams, every person has a role. A tank cannot move without a driver, nor can it fire without a gunner or load without an operator, and a tank can't do any of those things without a commander. The sum of the collective effort is greater than the sum of the individual parts and, like wolves, we are far stronger when we come together and work as a team for the good of the pack. Loyalty is the glue that binds individuals into teams, and strengthens bonds between peers. This loyalty is earned through professionalism, humility, decency and integrity, and an excellent team is one that feels good about itself and believes in its mission, and in its ability to succeed; we call this morale or team spirit. As Charles Darwin wisely noted, 'In the long history of humankind (and animal kind), those who learned to collaborate and improvise most effectively have prevailed'.

FINDING YOUR 'WHY'

In the Battle of Dunkirk in 1940, an outgunned British Expeditionary Force unit was isolated from its allies and faced inevitable annihilation as it was pinned between the English Channel and a narrow stretch of northern France. The soldiers were given a mission: to remain and fight, and to protect their fellow troops who were evacuating on the beach. They knew they were probably going to either die or be captured, but their regimental spirit, the power of the team and their respect for their leader who told them: *This is important* gave them an unshakeable sense of purpose. The strength of this purpose transformed their mission into a selfless and noble goal: to work for a greater collective good and to save the lives of others.

Fortunately, once word had reached them, their seafaring brothers back in England were quick to reciprocate as all manner of non-military vessels – from ferries to fishing boats – made their way over the Channel, like sitting ducks to the Luftwaffe, to save their fellow countrymen. While many were operated by naval officers, many of the other boats were sailed by their owners – ordinary people who were inspired to heroic acts of their own by the bravery of the trapped soldiers.

Field Marshal The Viscount Slim, who is remembered for his leadership and skill in restoring the morale of his soldiers when faced with a disastrous situation in Burma during the Second World War, believed that morale was a state of mind. For him, morale was the intangible force that could move a whole group of men to give their last ounce to achieve something, without counting the cost to themselves. He knew that morale helped make people feel they were part of something greater. The philosopher Friedrich Nietzsche once said: 'He who has a why to live can bear almost any how.' Purpose, the reason why you do what you do, is vital. And when the morale drops in a team, it is the sense of purpose that, when reinvigorated, can win the day.

It can sometimes be difficult to deliver good leadership when you're personally facing a tough moment and morale is low. For me, this came during an exercise when I needed to inspire my demoralised team – at a time when I myself felt utterly spent and void of morale...

GIVING YOUR BEST WHILE YOU'RE FEELING YOUR WORST

I was on BATUS in Canada as Commanding Officer of the First Fusiliers Battle Group. We had gone through the majority of the BATUS rotation and we were going into 'Totalise' – the final test exercise when the gloves come off from the free-playing Opposing Force (OPFOR). By that point, we were all completely shattered, having lived out of our vehicles throughout several tough weeks of training, with only snatches of sleep. The Totalise exercise consisted of a series of seven missions over a ten-day period. The first mission had gone really well, but in the second mission we were utterly taken apart. It was a defensive exercise, and we'd been digging trenches and vehicle scrapes to protect our equipment for over twenty-four hours. Our whole plan was carefully coordinated to ensure we had every possible angle covered. But the OPFOR found a route through us that we hadn't seen or covered. Frankly, it was humiliating. They literally drove through us because I hadn't planned properly. The stakes were high and, if this exercise had been for real, many of us would have been killed.

We then had to gather ourselves together, and go into an offensive set of missions. There was a period, during the switch of phase (the moment we received orders for our next mission), when I was literally falling asleep standing up. The Canada exercise is designed to test our ability to live and work under realistic combat conditions. This involves us living in the field for over a month and then being deprived of sleep during the actual missions. Everyone gets extremely tired and is pushed to the threshold of failure. The exercise is purposely made to be incredibly difficult to endure because being in a conflict is rarely easy. Better to experience it here first and learn how to cope, than in a conflict against a hostile force.

We were a demoralised battalion who felt like the bottom had dropped out of our world. We'd all hoped for success, but at that point we were clearly and unquestionably an unsuccessful battalion. I had to stand in front of the battlegroup and motivate them to give their best. The situation required every ounce of my leadership. Before addressing my battalion, I took a moment to gather myself and thought of the teachings of General Montgomery, one of the most prominent and successful British commanders of the Second World War: *Morale depends on leadership, discipline, comradeship and self-respect. Good morale is impossible without good leaders.*

I felt that my men were looking to me for the example. If I stood in front of them looking like I was beaten, then they would think we all were. I therefore took some time to make myself look as presentable as possible. There is definitely something to be said for standing straight and looking confident.

With Montgomery's words echoing in the back of my mind, I directly appealed to the soldiers' professional pride, focusing on values of comradeship and self-respect. I wasn't concerned about the personal career implications of failing that mission. Instead, I focused on the reputation of the battalion and the legacy of the Fusiliers regiment. I knew that if we failed too many missions then we would not be passed as combat-ready. We wanted to be among those deployed to Iraq a few weeks later, and we wanted to be given a good role. During these exercises, the Brigade Commander was effectively marking his battlegroups to work out which ones he could most trust to carry out the more difficult roles on operations. Professionally and personally, we all wanted our battlegroup to get a good role when the time came.

The reputation of the First Fusiliers Battle Group was something every soldier and officer alongside me had a stake in safeguarding. Upholding the Fusilier legacy became our *why*. There was a job that needed doing and we had to do it well because of that age-old Fusilier pride. Soldiers do not let their mates down and they certainly do not let the previous generation down by allowing their regiment's reputation to be tarnished. There was nothing in my speech that was rocket science. I just appealed to them to remember that they were part of something greater than themselves, which is something I'd learned to do as a junior officer all those years ago, during my first five weeks at Sandhurst. How important that sense of pride in the regiment is. How there's nothing worse than letting their friends or their regiment down.

There is a reason we encourage the cadets to soak up the atmosphere and history of Sandhurst. Its fine old buildings, its monuments, the beautiful Indian Army Memorial Room bathed in ethereal stained-glass light, the battle paintings on the wall, the sabres, the hallowed carved names of those who perished on the battlefield, the statues dotted around the grounds . . . They are all totems of tradition and legacy to which the officers-to-be bind themselves, and this legacy becomes a part of Sandhurst's reassuring fabric, with its roots – now part of their roots – stretching back to 1812. Regimental spirit is a powerful factor in creating strong morale. If soldiers feel invested in the tradition and fabric of their regiment, the more they will be spurred on by their best selves to protect its legacy. They feel part of something bigger than themselves.

THE BEST POLICY

Honesty is, I believe, the most important aspect of leadership. If you are straight with your people, they start to trust you and, once trust has been established, loyalty emerges and a close bond is formed. Honesty is all about character. You could call it authentic leadership: turning your character and personality into something your team can believe in and trust. In *Serve to Lead*, the officer cadet's little red bible of military wisdom, compiled in 1947, the following passage emphasises just how powerful being truthful can be:

> No amount of ability, knowledge or cunning can ever make up for not being straight. Once those under them find out that a commander is absolutely straight in all their dealings with them, they will love him as their leader, trust him, work for them, follow them and – should occasion arise – die for them.

Wherever you are, be it on the battlefield or in an office, the people you work alongside need to feel secure in the knowledge that they can really trust you. If you expect them to do something extraordinary, whether that means risking their lives against great odds in a conflict, or working late on an important project with no available overtime pay to reward them, they need to believe in you and the overall goal. In order to inspire others to go the extra mile, you need to give them a clear vision of *where* you want the team or project to go, *why* the goal is important, and *how* vital each of them is to achieving that goal.

At the end of the last millennium, philanthropist Bill Gates sagely remarked, 'As we look ahead into the next century, leaders will be those who empower others.' Empowering is tantamount to trusting your people and, at Sandhurst, we encourage all our cadets to recognise their strengths, and to keep developing themselves, because as leaders they should never be content with standing still or letting themselves stagnate. We often take the decision-making to the point where the information is. In other words, we allow the people closest to the question to answer it, trusting in their experience and specialist knowledge. To get the best out of officer cadets, we embrace the idea that everyone is a leader and has a view on how a problem should be tackled or a task carried out.

Trust works best when it flows both ways, and the art of a great leader lies in listening to those around you, consulting with them, deciding on the best course of action and then leading the way forward. In the past, there's no question that soldiers put their heads down and followed blindly. However, today's soldier is better connected, knows more and therefore has more questions and is not afraid to put their hand up and offer their input. If you find yourself managing a team, try to create a culture where everyone feels confident enough to share their own ideas, especially when you don't have any of your own yet. Be flexible enough to listen to others' suggestions – after all, you don't have a monopoly on ideas. As a manager, the final call will ultimately rest with you, but let your people know that you trust their creativity, experience and input. People need to feel empowered to use their initiative and come up with creative solutions. As a commanding officer, it's imperative that the people I'm leading feel like they can trust me – but I also need to trust them in return; their capabilities and their judgement. Every so often, situations will arise when there won't be time to consult or confer on the best course of action. Sometimes a window for success can seem small and, when it starts closing, your team must know that they have the freedom to seize an opportunity – to use their initiative and make a decision in the moment – and that you will back them.

Allow me to end on an instructive example of what we call 'daring initiative' while I was in Canada on yet another training exercise. We had an organisation within the battalion known as 'snipers' or sharpshooters, and their job was to sneak into the enemy's position, get behind their defences and cause pandemonium. We used lasers instead of bullets – for obvious reasons – but once a laser hit you, you were considered dead and could no longer take part in the exercise. It was a bit like playing a giant game of Laser Quest. Anyway, two of our snipers managed to get within fifty metres of the enemy headquarters undetected. One of them then tried to call in air support to take out the headquarters but there was no signal and the radio didn't work. Now, most people would have called it a day and given up, but not this guy. Though the radio had failed him, he had a mobile phone and, as he knew no Canadian numbers, he rang the Guard Room at the entrance of our army camp back in Germany, which was being manned 24/7 by a Rear Party while the battalion was away. The sniper called the Guard Room from almost 6,000 miles away and said, 'Here is the grid reference of the enemy's location, can you please get this to HQ in Canada?'

To cut a long story short, our friends in Germany did manage to relay those coordinates to us and we were able to engage the enemy and win the exercise. There is a 'Guard Room in Germany' solution for every problem; you just have to trust yourself and your team to find it.

How Do You React When Things Go Wrong?

Life's most valuable lessons are often learned when we leave our familiar comfort zones. Once we move into uncharted territory, we can really discover more about ourselves and grow. However, it's only natural that, in these strange places, we can sometimes find ourselves lost. It's easy to lose confidence and feel like other things are quickly spiralling out of our control. Similarly, when our cadets are high up in the Brecon Beacons, in freezing weather and blanketed in fog, one rocky outcrop starts to look like very much like all the others in the low visibility and, before they know it, they have become hopelessly disoriented. It is at moments like this – when we lose sight of our path, and our sense of direction – that we can take measure of ourselves, for better or worse, both as leaders and as people.

At Sandhurst, we teach cadets how to find their way, both practically and figuratively. Practically, we teach navigation; how to get from A to B using a map and compass. In this age of satellite navigation – of watches that can tell you which way to go and apps that can direct and guide – some find it strange that we go back to basics, but plotting a course is a basic leadership skill. Your soldiers will expect you to guide and lead them, by day and night, through fog and under fire. At the Academy, we start by teaching the basic navigational principles like using a compass, calculating a route time, and understanding contour lines, before moving on to individual navigation across the training area at the back of the Academy, known as Barossa. Many residents of Camberley will have their own tales of being asked, *Which way to the back gate?* by hot-and-bothered cadets staring helplessly at an upside-down map!

But getting yourself lost is the least of your issues. The main test at Sandhurst is when you're placed in a position of authority, charged with navigating for your section, patrol or platoon. Now you are the one responsible for not getting your entire team lost – and the one to blame if a wrong turn is taken. That kind of pressure continues throughout your career. I have personally endured many a sweaty map-reading moment of this sort, be that in the backstreets of Belfast, or the prairie in Canada, or leading my company of Warrior armoured vehicles (all fifteen of them) down a dead-end road in Germany. Not getting lost really is a key leadership skill.

We teach cadets to navigate using waypoints or rendezvous points (RVs). We use these points along the route to pause and check the map, as well as to check in with the rest of our team. They provide an opportunity to ensure we are well set for the next leg of our journey and confirm we are still heading in the right direction. But what happens if you become lost? Well, at Sandhurst we teach that you should always try and find your way back to the last RV – the most recent place you knew for sure where you were. That way, you gain the confidence of knowing you are no longer lost, and then you can re-check your compass and map, and get back on the correct route. Admitting you are lost and moving back to the last RV takes courage – it's sometimes embarrassing and hard to admit when you're wrong, especially if you have a whole platoon of soldiers following you.

FINDING YOUR WAY

In life we often take routes that appear to be leading us in the right direction, but then the weather changes, storm clouds form and these routes can all of a sudden lead to dead ends, or painful sudden drops. Whether it is a relationship, a career or a larger ambition that you feel has gone off-track, remember that getting lost is sometimes part of the journey to finding your way to where you want to be. The first thing to do is not to panic; take a second and breathe. Remember, a lack of breath sends a message to the brain to release more cortisol, the stress hormone. Don't let your thinking race ahead of you so that you start catastrophising – *I'm never going to get out of this . . . I'm going to be stuck here forever* – you will find a way and you won't be stuck. Stay calm. Take a look at your surroundings and try to find a waypoint. Since pre-historic times, walkers have built cairns (mounds of stones neatly piled on top of each other, usually on mountain peaks and hillside ridges). Though they have historically had some ceremonial purposes, cairns are now primarily used as trail markers, to help modern-day walkers find their bearings and orientate themselves in the landscape. Some walkers even add their own stone to the pile, to celebrate reaching this point on their journey as well as making sure the cairn remains solid for future walkers.

Using these cairns as markers, walkers can find their way back to a distinctive and reassuring landmark along their route, should they get lost and need to retrace their path.

Similarly, if you feel you've lost your way, and life has taken you far from the place you hoped you would be, take heart. It's never too late to get yourself back on track. Being lost is actually a positive, because it forces you to take time to assess where you are, where you want to be, and maybe realise that it's time to leave a place, job or person you're not happy with. This realisation is the first step to your finding your way to the right path towards your destination. If you start to feel lost, try to think back to the last time you felt you knew *where* you were and *who* you were, and examine it. What was good about it? Maybe you were exercising more, or spending more (or less) time with friends and family. Were you busy with plans for the future? Did you feel you had a clearer sense of purpose? Which of the people around you helped you feel positive? These introspective questions can guide you back to find the time when you started to feel yourself losing your way.

Now you know what that waypoint and mindset looked like, plot it on your mental map and slowly head back there, picking up useful habits that perhaps you've put down since that time. From this safe spot you can now reset yourself – take a rest, take care of yourself and start planning where you want to go, clearly mapping your destination. If it seems like a faraway place, break the journey down into regular waypoints. Never leave a waypoint until you have a plan of where you're going next, otherwise you'll keep getting lost in the mist. And as a stone of recognition for each that you reach, give yourself a pat on the back for getting this far, because each waypoint is taking you closer to where you want to be.

CHECK YOUR MORAL COMPASS

Sandhurst demands that we live by the army's values, and some would say that courage is the pre-eminent of these. Physical courage is required by all soldiers; few careers demand a contract of unlimited liability which asks an individual to, if necessary, lay down their life for a cause. For army leaders, physical courage is required to overcome fear, fatigue and hardship, to be able to stand and say, *Follow me*. But it is not just about physical courage. Moral courage is required to make the right decision, even if that might be unpopular with those you lead, such as admitting you are lost and need to move back to the last RV. Understanding the importance of values-based decision-making is a fundamental requirement of cadets at Sandhurst. We are constantly testing their ability to decide under pressure, checking to ensure their moral compass is as accurate as their actual prismatic one.

In 2003, I was a Company Commander during Operation Telic. Having fought our way into the Iraqi city of Basra, we found ourselves confronted by chaos. The enemy had melted away into the local population, the police force had been dissolved, and services, including medical care, were sporadic at best. We found ourselves trying to stabilise an increasingly complex situation and, as the local population started looting, we were tasked with bringing things under control.

The UN food distribution warehouse, on the outskirts of the city, was a particular focus of looting at the time. Within the warehouse, a separate group of soldiers from the larger battlegroup had been tasked with protecting the food stores. The soldiers, confronted by looters, looked for guidance from their leader, but he made a poor decision, resulting in the mistreatment of prisoners. That particular leader had lost sight of their moral compass and thereby allowed totally inappropriate behaviour to occur under their command.

My company had been tasked with patrolling the battlegroup's detained prisoners elsewhere in the city, and so our company were assumed to be the ones responsible for the mistreatment of the looters. I was immediately summoned to see my commander, who told me to find out who was responsible.

I went back to the base and – I'm ashamed to say it – in that moment my first thought was for myself: *That's it, then, that's the end of my career, my people have let me down.* Despite knowing in my heart that the people in my company would never do anything like this, I automatically assumed that what the commander said was true. They had let me down and, as a consequence, I was going to be punished. As I started to set about the painful and onerous task of weeding out the culprits, one of my Fusiliers came to see me and said, earnestly, 'It's not us. Trust me, it's not us.' And, of course, he was right. It was a completely different company of soldiers. Later, those responsible for the mistreatment were rightly court-marshalled and dishonourably discharged. In that moment with the Fusilier, I suddenly realised that, despite the fact that my men and I had been fighting side-by-side in Iraq for the last couple of months and the bonds of trust and comradeship we had developed over the years before, I had leapt to conclusions and not trusted my gut.

To this day, I regret that I so readily chose to mistrust my people, instead of defending them. I lost my way for a moment, and in doing so I almost lost the esteem of my team. Those soldiers would have done anything for me and I didn't stand up for them when it counted. If you take care of your team and stand up for them when it counts, your career will take care of itself. You'll be successful because you've built a bond of trust and you're running a happy ship. If you are the sort of person who thinks about their career at the cost of all else, then you may well lose your way. As a wise soul once advised me as I was about to assume command of a unit: 'Treat this as your last job in the army. Don't think about what comes next, just put every ounce of yourself into it and enjoy it.'

THE ARMY LEADERSHIP CODE

The army has developed a way of ensuring that leaders can translate the values they stand for – their moral compass – into leadership behaviours. At Sandhurst, cadets are debriefed on leadership decisions and actions based on the Army Leadership Code. It is a sort of codified 'checklist' to help you navigate your way.

Lead by Example
Encourage Thinking
Apply Reward & Discipline
Demand High Performance

Encourage Confidence in the Team
Recognise Individual Strengths & Weaknesses
Strive for Team Goals

The Army Leadership Code, whilst not quite a 'checklist' in the sense of a list of yes/no questions, is all about making sure you have thought about each of the elements and applied them to your leadership. These characteristics are what the Army expects from our leaders, and what we know works.

Every day presents fresh challenges for us all, and if you struggle and get lost, try to retrace your steps to where you know you were last on track. If you go off the rails and you lose your direction, there is *always* a way back; try to find the real you and the values you stand for. In true Socratic fashion, examine your actions, know yourself, get to know what works for you and, conversely, your triggers and how to avoid them. If you lose your job, rather than rushing to get another one immediately, stop and check in with yourself: Where are you? When was the last time you felt fulfilled in your work? Retrace to a time you didn't feel lost, and map that territory.

To avoid getting lost as a leader, set yourself goals and markers, RVs or waypoints if you will. Continually check your navigation and ask yourself if you are on track to reach your desired RV. Don't kid yourself you're perfect or beyond change; check in with your team, a friend or a mentor, on how you're doing, and create a regular dialogue of feedback. *How am I doing? How can I improve?* Checking in on your leadership means understanding your blind spots as well as your strengths. Once you've found them, the trick is then doing something about them.

Cadets at Sandhurst mark one another on how each performs on an exercise, particularly when they're in a position of authority. This means they get constant feedback on how they are doing. They learn to become comfortable with these appraisals – positive and negative – and we encourage them to improve and develop. The more successful you want someone to be, the more time you need to invest in them. Make sure you create an environment where people feel it's OK to reach out for help and feedback. In order to improve, we all need pointers on where we are going wrong. This might take the form of a mentor, a coach or more formal leadership development.

I have noticed some civilian organisations recruit and promote people based on their capability. As those individuals get more senior in the organisation, they are often placed in positions of leadership responsibility; senior roles for which they are not always equipped, because they have not had the opportunity to develop as leaders beforehand. No wonder they don't immediately flourish. The Army recognises leadership potential from an early stage. At Sandhurst we select cadets based on that potential before developing the leader over forty-four weeks.

But that is just the foundation. We understand that leadership is a journey; you never stop learning. Leadership requires constant development as you prepare for the next job, next role or next challenge – RVs where you can check in to ensure you are ready for the next leg. When you get lost – and, believe me, you'll almost certainly get lost at some point – retrace your steps back to a waypoint and reset.

7. TAKE A KNEE

Trust in Your Own Judgement

On 22 March 2017, a car crashed into multiple innocent Londoners and tourists, killing and maiming as it raced across Westminster Bridge towards the Houses of Parliament. The terrorist then left the vehicle and ran towards Parliament, where he was confronted by PC Keith Palmer, whom he attacked with a knife before being shot dead by another police officer.

Mike Crofts, an ex-army officer who had completed multiple tours in Afghanistan, heard the commotion and, regardless of the threat of further attack and warnings from the police to retreat to safety, was one of several people that ran towards the incident to assist. He saw the attacker being shot and also saw the wounded officer fall to the floor. Mike raced over and assessed Keith Palmer's injuries, removing his outer clothing and taking control, telling police he had some combat medical training. Despite the fact Mike had finished his tour of Afghanistan some three and a half years earlier, he fell into his old medical trauma training, having dealt with wounded soldiers while serving in the Middle East. Officer Palmer's bleeding was severe, so Mike called for Helicopter Emergency Medical Services (HEMS), ordering others to apply heavy pressure to the wound. He was composed and ordered everybody to remain calm. Tony Davis, a former Senior Non-Commissioned Officer (SNCO), was also on the scene, and he and Mike started CPR upon Keith Palmer and his assailant.

Mike eventually handed over his casualty, and ran to wait for the helicopter emergency services so that they could get a proper and professional handover. When HEMS landed, Mike stayed with the wounded officer while he was treated by the surgeon. For their bravery and selfless actions that day, Mike Crofts and Tony Davis were both awarded the Royal Humane Society bronze medal. While others were running away screaming from the danger, Mike was running towards it, focused and ready. His ability to remain composed and calm, as the fog of panic closed in around others, allowed him to take a deep breath and force himself into what we at Sandhurst sometimes refer to as a 'Condor Moment'; a composed place where he wasn't propelled by fight or flight, but instead, could take a second to trust in his own judgement. He gave himself a snatch of time to quickly draw on what he'd learned at Sandhurst and from his wealth of experience accrued on the battlefield.

TAKE A CONDOR MOMENT

In a pressured conflict, it's imperative not to let your blood rule your brain. Instead of rushing in offensively with retaliation, stand back, take stock of the situation, reset, recalibrate and then act. The term Condor Moment has its origins in a series of dry-humoured commercials for Condor pipe tobacco in the 1980s, where a pipe smoker variously and deftly deals with whomever is ruining the peace of his meditative smoke. Admittedly, the term might be showing its age a little (!) and you don't have to smoke a pipe, or even have been in the army, to apply this transformative skill to your everyday life. All it requires is a presence of mind to take a moment to consider your options and plan your next step. A Condor Moment could last as long as a few days or as little as a few seconds, if that is all you have. The important thing is to allow yourself the thinking space to make a decision when faced with urgency. In a crisis, you might not think you have time to spare, but I can assure you that a few precious moments for contemplation are almost always valuable and justified.

Our more generic term for taking time out in a dangerous area or 'hot zone' is: 'take a knee'. This saying derives from getting down on one knee and lowering your position to avoid live fire as it zips over your head. Stepping back from the situation, taking a breath and letting the adrenalin dissipate is vital. In the midst of a crisis, it's important to remember that you are not alone – you have your team around you, you know each other's strengths and weaknesses, and you have your training to fall back on. As a leader, backing yourself is crucial when you're under pressure. Sandhurst helps you trust that you have the right material and qualities to deliver in a tight situation.

In moments of crisis, it's your job as a leader to invigorate your team with certitude, confidence and to give them hope, assuring them they are the best people to overcome the challenge and that you believe in them. The rest is details. If they believe that you have faith in them, they will have faith in themselves. In November 1915, Ernest Shackleton and his crew found themselves in desperate straits when their ship *Endurance* became trapped and crushed by an ice floe in the Antarctic wilderness. They needed to find their way back to civilisation before they starved to death or succumbed to the harsh Antarctic conditions. Stranded on the ice sheet with death waiting in the wings, Shackleton spoke to his men calmly, confidently and strongly. 'He told us', recalled one of the crew years later, 'that we ought to march five miles a day, and that if [we] all worked together it could be done. We were in a mess and the Boss [Shackleton] was the man who could get us out.' In April 1916, Shackleton set out by lifeboat from Elephant Island with just five of his crew, crossing 1600 km of treacherous ocean to reach South Georgia in the hopes of finding help. After trekking across the island, they reached the whaling station at Stromness, and finally, in August 1916, the other members of Shackleton's crew were brought to safety. Against incredible odds, every member of the *Endurance* expedition had survived.

COOLER HEADS PREVAIL

A few years after passing out from the Academy, I went off to fight in the First Gulf War. I had been in Northern Ireland before, during the Troubles, but I'd never been in a proper combat zone. Suddenly life was moving at 100 mph. One moment we were in Germany painting the vehicles a sandy colour; the next we were training in the desert; soon we were getting our soldiers ready to go, and then we were off and heading into Saudi Arabia, moving up to the front. We had an hour or so waiting for the artillery to do its thing before we could move forward, and that's when all these doubts and fears started to slither and form in my mind. When you have the luxury of time and the opportunity to think, you start ruminating about the unexpected. We didn't know what was going to happen. We'd heard there were chemical threats. But then I reminded myself that I had got this far and that I just needed to take a Condor Moment. The answers were in there somewhere.

One night we left FUP Green, on the Iraq border, in the early hours of the morning. It was very dark and, although we didn't realise it yet, we were starting to experience the effects of the burning oil platforms like sore throats, headaches and dizziness. My platoon was leading the battlegroup's advance and our job was to ensure the route to the Objective Brass was clear of any enemy forces. Once there, we were to mark a new FUP from which the battlegroup would launch its attack. I was navigating the twelve-vehicle group using our newly issued satellite navigation system that was the size of a small suitcase. We were moving quickly, and my face was glued to the small navigation screen telling me which direction to go. This was not the time to get lost.

After an hour or so, one of my vehicles came up on the platoon radio net and gave a Sighting Report. They had seen something up ahead. The Platoon immediately slowed as we began to try to work out what it was. More information surfaced: it was a group of armoured vehicles moving across our front. The Milan (anti-tank missile) section asked me for permission to fire, but a voice in the back of my head told me to stop. Don't ask me why, but maybe it was my Sandhurst 'take a knee' training telling me to think this through. The obvious thing would be to engage but they were presenting no significant threat and they showed no signs of having seen us. I forwarded the sighting report to the battlegroup Headquarters, explained what we were seeing, and they told me to engage if the vehicles presented a threat to us or the route. I decided to move forward to investigate further and, as we did, we saw that they were indeed armoured personnel carriers, very similar to our own 432 variant. We held our fire. Moving closer still, and they looked worryingly similar to our own vehicles. I asked Headquarters if there were any 'friendly' units in our vicinity. They replied that there weren't. Still, we did not fire.

Eventually, one of the platoon vehicles managed to get a good visual through the early-morning gloom and we discovered they were indeed friendly vehicles: an Armoured Field Ambulance section from a neighbouring unit had become lost in the night and found themselves way ahead of where they were scheduled to be. I was so thankful that I had given myself time to think before rushing in.

In the onset of a predicament, whether it's a firefight in a hot zone, or a sudden problem in the workplace, it's important to stop and take yourself out of the situation. Catch your breath, and approach the problem evenly by 'taking a knee'. Even the best of us can get drawn into a fight sometimes, but it's when we collect ourselves that we're at our optimum and can make the best decisions. Rely on your training and those around you, and come up with a plan. And always think before you rush in. One of my Colour Sergeants recently told me a story about when he was serving under a young officer in Afghanistan: 'My Platoon Commander in Helmand was a 24-year-old officer – youthful and a little inexperienced but possessed of a natural authority. When our platoon was all gung-ho and eager for a fight with the Taliban, he had the maturity to know when to encourage this and when not to . . . Protecting his men was his absolute priority, and thanks to his cool head and sound judgement the whole platoon came back alive.'

THINKING UNDER PRESSURE

When somebody first learns to box, the common experience is that they 'freeze' on receiving the first blow, their legs turning to jelly. The reason for this is they're producing so much of a stress chemical known as cortisol, that the body shuts down, or veers towards 'flight', i.e. running away. The other likelihood is the person will produce too much testosterone, 'see red' and start throwing poorly positioned punches as they are seized by the urge to 'fight'. The body will only go to such extremes in situations when it feels threatened and, as a boxer learns to cultivate their fighting craft with block and counter techniques to protect them, their body quickly gets used to the stressful situation of taking a punch and it no longer feels the need to initiate its fight and flight responses. The boxer becomes calmer and is able to reason under the attack, picking their shots carefully, not losing their temper or their breath to panic.

If you apply this to any crisis, isn't it better to avoid being hot-headed and throwing caution to the wind, and instead to take a moment to figure out your best option? When Panamanian boxer Roberto Durán shocked the world and beat Sugar Ray Leonard in Montreal in 1976, he did so with tenacity, fiery brutality and relentless force. But he had begun his mental offensive a few days earlier, before the fight, having psychologically got to Ray by threatening him in a nearby park while he was with his wife. This brought out the fight instinct in Ray, and so he was angry and fell straight into Durán's plan. They fought toe-to-toe like a couple of streetfighters trading punches. This style of fighting played to Durán's strengths; he was in his element and he won conclusively – but their next bout was very different. Leonard fought his own fight his own way, not getting angry, boxing from a distance, orchestrating his combinations and picking his punches thoughtfully. There was no fight or flight behaviour any more. A very frustrated Durán threw in the towel and uttered the words that became forever infamous in the canon of boxing: *No mas!* ('No more!') The lesson here is that it's always better to have a plan and stick to it, rather than losing your cool in the moment.

Back in the Gulf, my platoon was tasked with leading the battlegroup on another night move – this time we had to find a crossing point over an oil pipeline which cut across the battlegroup's axis of advance, obstructing the route forward. We had been joined by Royal Engineers, whose technical expertise would help us get our platoon and vehicles over the pipeline, and consequently we now had an even bigger group of vehicles to manoeuvre through the darkness. Intelligence had told us about a number of suitable crossing points and I already had a couple of options programmed into my sat nav. As we approached the first crossing point, I received a sighting report of unknown vehicles positioned on and around the crossing point. As I waited for more detail, tracer rounds illuminated the night as someone opened fire. Confusion reigned as I tried to find out who was firing and at what. My mind was racing and I felt a real urgency that I ought to do something at once – *right or wrong, make a decision* – but then a different, calmer voice in my head told me to take a pause. I kept listening as the platoon's vehicle commanders talked to one another on the radio, painting a picture of what was going on. While I was listening in, I checked with Battle Group HQ to rule out the presence of friendly vehicles. The rest of my platoon quietly got on with what they had been trained to do, established that this was indeed enemy fire and began to fight back. The enemy bunkers and buildings, as they turned out to be, were kept at bay, while the Engineers marked the crossing points to guide the rest of the battlegroup over the pipeline. Despite the initial confusion, all went relatively smoothly; this was something we had practised many times before. Everyone knew what to do and everyone trusted one another to get on and do it, and so while the rest of my team got on with the job at hand, I was able to 'take a knee', properly control the situation and coordinate our efforts. By stepping back and listening, I gave myself space to think about the 'what next' and avoided being stuck simply reacting to the 'right now'.

Remaining calm as a leader, especially when you find yourself in hot water, requires a level of mental resilience – but when you stay calm, others will be calmed too. Likewise, a display of panic will be reflected back in the behaviour of your team. So goes the saying: 'Ten soldiers wisely led will beat a hundred without a head.' When you're confronted by the unexpected or the unfamiliar, give yourself a second and let your mind catch up instead of rushing headfirst into it. Whether it's 'taking a knee' or a taking a Condor Moment, if you give yourself the space to think, you can find the solution in yourself. The answer is always there.

8. TRAIN HARD, FIGHT EASY

Fail to Prepare and Prepare to Fail

One of the hardest physical and mental tasks cadets are put through during their time at Sandhurst comes in the eighth week of their first term: 'Exercise Long Reach'. It takes place in tough mountain terrain in the Welsh Brecon Beacons, where the weather is unrelenting. In summer, there is no cover from the sun; during the winter months, the temperature drops below freezing. Such a dangerous environment pushes people to the limits of their physical and mental endurance.

Over a thirty-two-hour period, our officer cadets must navigate their way around ten patrolled and five unpatrolled checkpoints in groups of four. They each carry their heavy 20kg Bergen on their back and walk between 60 and 70 km through bogs, fast-flowing streams, fields of 'babies' heads' (rocky clumps of earth and grass), high slippery slopes and fast-falling veils of mist. Depending on the time of year, the risk of hypothermia or heatstroke waits spectrally in the wings. On successful completion of Long Reach, cadets are left feeling hugely empowered by the realisation of just how deep their reservoirs of endurance and grit can run when they are feeling pushed to their absolute limit. With this new self-knowledge, they no longer carry around the same unhelpful doubts about their own abilities or fears of failure, and approach future tasks and exercises with far greater confidence.

OUT-THINKING YOUR OPPONENT

At Sandhurst, we make our training as difficult and complex as possible, so cadets have a kind of muscle memory that kicks in when faced with the real thing. There's an old Maori saying: *Train to win, practise under pressure*, and our officer cadets definitely get more than their fair share of pressure. Through practice and training, cadets can move certain actions from the conscious to the sub-conscious, so that when the time comes they happen almost on instinct and without conscious or deliberate thought. Drills are a vital part of achieving this, but we should not aim to set all our actions to auto-pilot — otherwise we would spend a lot of time reacting, instead of planning a more far-sighted response. We still remind cadets that they will need to anticipate and plan for the third bend down the road, not just the first.

For example, if an IED (Improvised Explosive Device) goes off, there is every chance that the enemy will have placed a second ary device where they think we will be most likely to gather our survivors together before ushering them to safety. We teach our cadets to second-guess the enemy's attempt to predict our reaction. By anticipating our opponents' behaviours, we can prepare for them, and out-think them with our response. We also build worst-case scenarios and prepare for them, thinking, *What is the enemy's most dangerous course of action and what do I have to do to combat it?* We encourage cadets to weigh up their options first, before wading into a situation. If, having done so, they make the right decision, we unpick their success afterwards with feedback from others — what worked and why, and how might we improve upon it next time? In business, it's common practice to get together to have a team discussion when things are bad and problems need addressing, but imagine if you were to meet more frequently when things were going well. What if you took time to identify the key factors of a success and find out what exactly it is that's making everything tick along so smoothly? I know everyone says that failure is a great teacher, but that doesn't mean that we can't also learn valuable lessons from our moments of success.

If we are to succeed in our mission to defend, our forces need to constantly adapt, always mindful of the fact that tomorrow's war will be different – but no less complex – to ones before it. In order to rise to and meet this challenge, we have to second-guess the future and plan for it. We imagine our foe at their most destructive and dangerous worst, in order to be our best. It would be easy to rest on our laurels and think we've got it covered, but the face of warfare is evolving rapidly. Imagine drones in the Battle of the Somme, or tanks at the battle of Agincourt – yesterday's impossibles are fast becoming today's realities as technology continues to develop at breakneck speed. It's also important to remember that new methods can have both a positive and a negative application. We can use drones to help save the lives of our soldiers, because we can use them to carry out reconnaissance in potentially 'hot' areas where previously we would have needed soldiers on the ground and might have incurred fatalities. However, drone technology can also be used to do harm, with some drones armed with weapons that can be fired remotely at an enemy. Technological advances are accessible to the highest bidder, with little thought to what they might ultimately be used for.

Even during peacetime, we must constantly be ready for war, and that means training to our absolute limit so that, when the time does come to face the enemy, the actions are ingrained in us and we are fit for the fight. We train hard to ensure that everyone knows their role, responsibilities and movements – where they are going and what they are doing – come the real event. We drum the training on the proper handling of weapons into our cadets so thoroughly that they are able to operate them when under pressure, even in total darkness. In war, repetition and practice are the seeds of victory. Muhammad Ali's words are as applicable today as they were when he spoke them almost half a century ago: 'The fight is won or lost far away from witnesses – behind the lines, in the gym, and out there on the road, long before I dance under the lights.'

FAIL TO PREPARE AND PREPARE TO FAIL

At Sandhurst, we teach that if you have time, you should always conduct rehearsals – especially if you are about to undertake a complex operation. Rehearsals mean that every man and woman has the chance to practise what they will do on the night; and they can see what everyone else will be doing and exactly where they will be. Timings can be rehearsed to make sure they're realistic and achievable and, perhaps most importantly, these give us a chance to 'what if' – to play through various scenarios and plan for contingencies.

As part of the preparations for the final attack into Basra in 2003, the First Fusiliers Battle Group found itself in defensive positions to the west of the city along the line of the Shatt al-Arab waterway. The orders were clear: we were to 'dominate no-man's land'. This involved a series of operations that were intended to tie down the enemy's resources and keep them guessing. The battle-group launched a series of offensive probes into the city over a period of roughly ten days, in order to elicit a reaction from the enemy that would reveal valuable information about their strength, positioning, and other useful tactical data.

At that time, Y Company was in reserve; we were taking a rest at the International Airport. Bridge 2, the key motorway bridge over the Shatt al-Arab river, was taking sporadic mortar fire from a couple of buildings within the city, and although Aviation had tried to deal with the threat, the fear of the potential collateral damage to civilians on the ground meant the only way to stop it was to launch a fighting patrol. Y Company was tasked with taking out the source of the mortar fire and, if possible, securing a prisoner for questioning. This was to be a company fighting patrol, consisting of Company Headquarters, 7 Platoon and the company's Manoeuvre Support Section (machine guns and snipers). We had time to prepare and so I gave a comprehensive set of orders to the whole patrol and then we practised.

The afternoon before the fighting patrol, we all went out onto the airfield and rehearsed the whole thing: how we were going to get to our destination, who would carry what, which actions we'd carry out on the objective, who would call for fire, who would take the prisoner . . . you get the point. Everything was covered, and we left nothing to chance. Then we ran through the various 'what ifs': what if we get lost, what if we have a casualty, what if the enemy is no longer there? By the end of all our preparation, I'm pretty sure my troops were sick to death of the whole operation – but they knew it off by heart, inside out and back to front. Like a dancer, they knew every step.

We went out that night and achieved our objective – and we brought back a prisoner. Nothing went wrong and we suffered no casualties. We were lucky – or was it that we had made our own luck? It wasn't just low-level operations like this that were rehearsed, prior to the initial attack into Iraq; the entire force, both US and UK, had conducted Receipt of Orders Drills. These consisted of a run-through of the operation using a huge model of the ground, enabling Commanders to get a feel for the size and scale of the operation; who would be on their left and right; who would be coming up from behind. It allowed us to check the synchronisation of the operation and confirm the coordination of our fires. And of course we went through the 'what ifs' to ensure everyone knew when and how the plan might need to change in the moment because, as the old adage goes: 'No plan survives contact with the enemy!'

DARING INITIATIVE

Rehearsals also give you the opportunity to ensure your people really understand the purpose of the operation – the 'why' – and, most importantly, what part they are to play in the plan. This drives disciplined initiative, allowing soldiers to act based on an understanding of the Commanders' intent. This empowerment is a constant theme throughout these chapters because it is vitally important. Good orders followed by good rehearsals help unlock good initiative.

On an armoured raid into Basra, my company had been tasked with taking out an enemy anti-aircraft gun that was dominating one of the routes into the city. The Company Group this time was made up of 9 Platoon and a troop of main battle tanks from B Squadron, Queen's Royal Lancers. In the orders, I had set an LOE (Limit of Exploitation), which essentially means I had drawn a line on the map beyond which we were not to advance. During our rehearsals, using a model for reference, we had discussed when people might need to go beyond that line and I'd explained how and in what scenarios we could afford to take such risks. On the operation itself, we reached the LOE without coming across our target. As I was ordering the withdrawal, one of our tank commanders spotted the anti-aircraft gun some way up ahead, as it was being dragged away and hidden from sight. Without waiting for permission, the Tank Commander took the initiative and seized the window of opportunity, advancing to engage the enemy. His training had drilled into him that risk was sometimes a healthy option and, after all our rehearsals, he knew the parameters in which he could use his 'daring initiative'. He felt empowered to listen to his gut and engage the enemy beyond the LOE because we had discussed and run through this eventuality – along with countless others – during our many rehearsals.

In the British Forces we spend most of our time preparing for major combat operations, and that also develops the right skill sets, discipline and standards that allow our soldiers to adapt to other tasks such as peacekeeping and humanitarian operations. At Sandhurst our training is designed to be testing – often more testing than the execution of real operations – and we teach the officer cadets how to think when they're in a tight situation through a range of drills: TTPs (Tactic Technique Procedures) or SOPs (Standard Operating Procedures). These routine, commonplace drills can be used instinctively in whatever situation the cadet might be faced with. By applying them, cadets can steady their heart rate, take a pause, or react to something in a practised and methodical way – reducing the amount of mental energy needed to generate a response for a specific moment. They know that they can use these familiar drills as a sort of guiding framework and, by leaning on their ingrained good habits, they are able to take actions in what might otherwise be a daunting situation. For instance, when faced with enemy fire for the first time, a vast majority of soldiers' instinctive reactions are disbelief and mental paralysis. This has always been the case and such scenarios can never truly be replicated through training or live-fire exercises. However, a soldier's training, self-confidence, and framework of drills can help them to counter-balance these reactions, serving as a reassuring handrail when, under pressure, they may feel like the ground has lurched out from under them.

Not everything in life will be easy, and we can all find ourselves confronted with complex problems in our day-to-day lives. As a leader, you can't afford to leave things to chance. Of course, in the army — and in everyday life — we don't always have the luxury of time to contemplate our options to the level we'd like, and sometimes we might have to rely on our training and experiences to see us through a tough spot. But, if we *are* able, we should try to take time and run things through to ensure we have everything lined up and ready. You might have a big presentation to make to your colleagues or a new client, a special event to plan, or an important job interview where you're keen to make a great impression. Take time to practise and run through scenarios, because considering a 'what if' is time well spent.

The Standard You Walk Past is the Standard You Accept

During the writing of this book, I've often asked myself just what are the special Sandhurst ingredients that are responsible for the multi-dimensional officers we forge here? Is it the values we teach them to live by, or the excellent mentoring that the cadets receive from their Colour Sergeants and the example they are set by their Platoon Commanders? Or is it the fine-tuning of their already promising characters? Perhaps it's the fact we teach them to face their fears and weaknesses, be they public speaking or field skills, to the point that they are no longer daunted by them. The answer is, it's probably all of them and many more besides. However, I do know with total confidence that, by the end of the first term, our cadets are already starting to think like soldiers and appreciating the benefits of working in a team. But what of their courage; their ability to take on huge tasks and somehow get through? And where do they learn that deeply entrenched sense of compassion inter-woven with steely determination, for which the British officer is celebrated and envied worldwide; that lack of hubris and sense of humour that separate them from all other forces?

Unable to answer these questions single-handedly, I appealed to a host of Sandhurst alumni and asked them to share what Sand-hurst had most impressed upon them. Did any of its teachings and wisdoms – or the multitude of diverse skills – still guide and sup-port their day-to-day lives? The response was quite overwhelming, and my sincere thanks go to all those who shared their stories with me. Sadly, there were limits to how many I could list within this little tome, and the following really are the tip of the iceberg.

Andrew Todd, MBE, mountaineer, active Lieutenant Colonel in the Royal Gurkha Rifles, presented with a Military Award for saving lives on Mount Everest

'At 6,000 feet, because of the lack of oxygen, your decision-making is diluted, and my frame of reference for who I was and a reminder of what I was made of always defaulted back to who I'd been at

Sandhurst. While there, I learned to continually strive to do the best for my team and others who might be in trouble, to do the right thing every day. When the earthquake shook Nepal on 25 April 2015, I was trying to put a serving Gurkha on the summit of Mount Everest to celebrate the 200th anniversary of the Gurkha Regiment. An avalanche ripped through Base Camp flattening everything in its path and killing eighteen people. Most of our team, including myself, were cut off at Camp 1, as the route back down was decimated. We were resting in our tents, eating and drinking, when the glacier under Camp 1 shook violently, crevasses opened up behind our tents and the mountains around us exploded. I couldn't hear anything except the earth below us and the mountain crashing above. The ground dropped beneath us with a swing from side to side, and as I put my head out of the tent I was hit by a cloud of snow; a blast wave from the massive avalanche that we later discovered had wiped out much of Base Camp.

'At Camp 1, we set about planning the rescue of the 120 climbers and Sherpas stranded at Camps 1 and 2. We had enough food for a few days. That night, the aftershocks got louder and triggered avalanches closer to our tents. We were sitting ducks and extremely thankful when we were extracted by helicopter and taken to Base Camp on the third day after the earthquake.

'Instead of leaving the dead on the mountain, my team and I felt compelled to do our bit and stayed on recovering bodies. Sandhurst taught me that despite adversity, I had the reserves to keep going, but I also knew when to pull back. Courage is a bank account: drive it to the edge of its overdraft but know when to stop spending; rest and let your men rest too. Mental wellness is about avoiding burnout, so rest, reset and recharge.

'A mountain strips you down to your basic raw materials. Survival is everything, but on Everest, my own survival was secondary to that of my men. I learned this too while at Sandhurst. I found it very hard to accept the *Sun* newspaper's Military Award for the most outstanding soldier, because of the ethos of being a team member which I also learned there.'

Luke Sinnott, para-athlete and former Royal Engineers Search Advisor

'At Sandhurst, they remould you into someone who possesses discipline, which doesn't come naturally. I learned there that if you're going to do something then do it right and give it 100 per cent. You can't be master of all trades but you can give it your best. During training we were sometimes given near-insoluble tasks to help us recognise that some situations were un-winnable and that failure cannot be helped, while other scenarios required you to take a Condor Moment and mentally step away from the intensity of the problem in order to decide on the best course of action. Sandhurst taught me to keep a level head and that there were always options. Before going to Afghanistan in 2010, I knew there was a very high risk factor that one of my Platoon would be injured, so I joked to my men that if anyone was to lose a leg they had to go to the Paralympics. On 20 November 2010, I was put into an induced coma because of the blast damage caused by an exploding IED (improvised explosive device) to my legs, both of which I lost. By Christmas that year, I decided I was going to try out for the Rio Paralympics. I thought sailing might be the best route to get there and I joined the GB solo sailing team in 2011. However, because Sandhurst had taught me such a strong sense of being a team player, this didn't really suit me.

'So I sat down and thought, *What else can I do?* And I decided on the long jump. During my time at Sandhurst, we learned a lot about goal setting and the need to deliberately plan what you will need to achieve your goal. Once I'd set that goal, I broke it down into smaller tasks, the first of which was to get hold of some blades to run on. In 2014 I started training, and by 2017 I was competent enough to make it to the World Para Athletics Championships. I remember I was coming eighth and was about to take my fifth jump when I decided to take a Condor Moment. Twenty thousand people were watching, it was the debut event, and I needed the support of the crowd to lift me. So I began a slow clap, which the crowd followed, and then I jumped. I ended up in fourth place. Sandhurst taught me how to cope under pressure like this.'

Vicki Wentworth, Chief Customer Officer, Wesleyan Assurance Society, ex-Squadron Commander

'Sandhurst builds on innate character, developing strengths and working on weaknesses. It also approaches problem solving and decision making in a very structured way. Compared with my peers in the workplace, I am much more likely to be comfortable going ahead with an 80 per cent plan, taking considered risks with a highly tuned sense of intuition. You don't always have the time to gather all the evidence before the opportunity may be gone, so apply intellect and judgement, use your experience, seek feedback, and then make a decision and move forward, ready to change the plan though if it begins to falter. Sandhurst taught me to analyse situations and to make big decisions quickly, rather than procrastinate, and to be intuitive and analytical in equal measure.

'Another aspect that set me apart in my professional life when I first left the military was that I was sometimes accused of not caring about things that hadn't gone to plan. It seemed that because I wasn't stressed and shouting like some of my colleagues, I wasn't as connected, but of course this wasn't the case; I just knew better how to deal with pressure. The negative behaviour that comes out under pressure doesn't help anything, neither your team, nor your productivity, nor moving towards a solution. Sandhurst helped me keep a cool head and taught me to step out of the emotion and problem-solve more effectively. By making me tackle areas of weakness within myself that I would otherwise have avoided, Sandhurst helped me become more rounded and multi-dimensional. It also gave me the confidence to be authentic and confident as a leader.'

Simon Dixon, consulting partner, Deloitte, ex-Major, Queen's Royal Lancers

'Sandhurst taught me that a good leader makes his subordinates successful, so they in turn make him successful. Juniors need to understand you, your seniors need to understand you, and your peers need to support you and help you navigate problems. Business can be stressful and you need to be able to take feedback and give it.

Also, you need to know when to apply the right leadership style at the right time; when to be directing with an overview, and when to be at the front at the coalface.

'Some of the characteristics that make a good officer are applicable for a good consultant too: presence, flexibility, a sense of humour, initiative, the ability to listen, balancing the well-being of your team with your goal, humility, positive thinking, calmness, trustworthiness, reassurance and bravery.'

Nicola Wetherill, MBE, explorer, active Major in the Royal Army Medical Corps

'In 2018, I was one of the six Ice Maidens, the first ever all-women team to ski the 1,700 km from coast to coast of the Antarctic via the South Pole, in temperatures of -50°C. In the selection process to find the other five team members, I was looking for people who would never give up. I remember when I was at Sandhurst I was quite competitive and pretty fit, and we were doing a run together, not a race, and one of the girls behind me was struggling and said to me breathlessly: 'I'm following your feet, Nics, I'm following your feet to keep going!' And that made me realise that she was relying on me, so instead of running to the front, following my competitive spirit, I decided to stay where I was so I could help her. At Sandhurst, you're always taught to put other people before yourself.

'There's a time to show yourself as an individual and a time to serve your team, so when we were choosing the Ice Maidens, it was important to find people who wanted to go to the South Pole for the team and not themselves. I didn't want to get someone who was over-competitive, but somebody who was honest and open. Up until the penultimate training exercises in Norway, I had presented myself as more of a leader than a human being, and one of the girls was wearying a bit and so I skied over to her and said, 'I don't know about you, but I'm tired,' and later she said to me, 'It was so nice to hear you say that because then I realised it was O K to say I too was tired in front of you, and it didn't mean that I was too weak to stay on the team.' Disclosing a little humility and human weakness made other people feel better. I think Sandhurst was responsible for teaching me humility and the ability to be open.

'When I go and talk to schools, I say to the girls, "Once, not long ago, I was a little girl sitting where you are, but you can't see the glass stairway, the seemingly impossible path I took to get here now – all the things that I had to do to get to the point where I was walking with my team of Ice Maidens through the Antarctic."

Sandhurst gives cadets a chance to really discover their strengths and weaknesses. It's a place where you learn that you can never stop improving yourself and no goal is too big for you. I came up with the idea to cross Antarctica because I'd heard someone talking about their experience of doing it, and he made the audience feel as if we could never do it. Afterwards, I went up to him and said, "How do I get involved in something like this?" and he replied, "I happened to be in the right place at the right time." Not very helpful, but it made me think, *Right, I'm going to create my own right place and right time*. It took me ten years to put my goal into action, so I say to kids: "Don't wait for things to happen. Be active, don't be passive." '

There are plenty of common themes in these testimonials: the importance of teamwork and never giving up; going the extra mile to succeed; and the importance of thinking ahead and 'taking a knee' to think things through. Initiative and keeping a cool head are also present, as are the common traits of inspiring others, and being positive and compassionate. The wide and flexible skillsets of these alumni, and their wealth of experiences mean that they could all respond to and succeed in a wide variety of challenges, adapting like a Swiss Army knife to meet the needs of a new situation. What also struck me was the richness of their lives, their determination to climb to the top of their careers armed with honesty and resourcefulness, or to court danger in some of the toughest places on earth, in the interests of challenging commonly held gender bias, or simply to save others.

Success is not measured by how many thousands of miles you've walked or climbed but in your daily actions towards those around you. Everyone casts their own leadership shadow and, when we find ourselves in positions of authority or power over others, that leadership shadow only grows and the more our actions and decisions have an impact on and influence the behaviour of those around us. We have to be the good example. We all have it in us to be heroic every day, to be less focused on ourselves and more aware of other's needs. Now, as we work our way towards the end of the book, I want you to start thinking about Standing Up Straight with regard to your inner moral compass, and ask yourselves how often you are 100 per cent true to your best self, or if on occasion you have turned the other cheek and walked past someone who was in trouble and needed your help. Maybe it was risky to get involved, and as others walked on by you chose to do the same. Perhaps it was a time you were offered a challenge or opportunity that you decided to pass on for fear of failure. We must remind ourselves that the standard we walk past is the standard we accept. It is never too late to change.

Courage, as we'll see in the next chapter, cannot easily be taught, but with the right response training, fear can be diminished. In fact, there are a great many things we can alter in ourselves without fundamentally changing who we are, just by following a few life tips from Sandhurst: goal setting, planning and taking pride in small details; punctuality, backing yourself, travelling light emotionally and physically; working as a team and practising self-awareness and resilience, taking time out under pressure for a Condor Moment, and training hard in order to be fight-fit. A leopard can't change its spots? Nonsense.

10. SERVE TO LEAD

The Power of Example

A Company Commander who was being deployed to Kenya waited for his heavily delayed plane to depart from Brize Norton, England, for fourteen hours. When the aircraft finally did leave, the flight took a further ten hours, which would then be followed by yet another ten hours of driving at the other side, in Kenya. On arrival, the Company Commander needed everything to be unloaded from the truck and placed in a hangar. Despite his long journey, he climbed into the vehicle and began unloading it himself. He had plenty of other things to do but wanted to lead by example. As he went to work, others immediately came to help him. After this episode, anything that he asked others to do, they happily did for him. Why? Because he led by example and served to lead.

If I had to choose a single principle that I consider central to being a good leader, I would say it is integrity, the ability to be honest with your people. Integrity fosters trust, the bedrock of every good team. The best way to earn this trust is by being true to yourself: to your personal values as well as to those that you and your team all live by. You might call it authentic leadership. It's about turning your personality and character into something people can believe in and trust. Integrity, trust and confidence are all intrinsically linked. If you have integrity, you will be trusted, which in turn breeds confidence in your team.

AUTHENTIC LEADERSHIP AND INFECTIOUS COURAGE

Sometimes all that is required to incentivise a flagging team is recognition of what they are going through. I remember during the Second Gulf War, a three-star general in charge of the whole US and UK expeditionary force turned up at the warehouse in Basra. We gathered around him and he acknowledged the difficult position we were in, and reminded us *why* we were there. He was also prepared to show a little vulnerability and told us that he was missing his family, just like the rest of us. Admissions like this make a leader more human and easier to relate to. I believed him; there was something authentic and honest in the way he carried himself and spoke, the directness of his gaze. He seemed to understand exactly what we were up against and empathised with us. The soldiers were riveted by his every word; I reckon they would have followed him anywhere. It was no great Churchillian speech, there was no rhetoric, no artistry of dramatic pauses or thundering crescendos; behind his uniform, this three-star general was still just a normal decent person, no different from the rest of us. But he really seemed to care about us. There was a visible change in everyone after that, a shifting of gears as they felt understood and appreciated.

To borrow a phrase from Field Marshall The Viscount Slim, 'It is not that the British soldier is braver than other soldiers. They are not – but they are brave for a bit longer, and it's that bit that counts.' Courage is the ability to act on your beliefs despite the danger or disapproval it might elicit. Courage has many forms: moral, physical, emotional, intellectual. Arguably, moral courage is the most important, as it guides us through what is wrong and what is right. Moral courage is often about feeling fear but having the willpower to push on despite this, trusting in yourself and in your abilities, as well as the other people in your team. Courage lives in all of us; however, some are able to access it more easily than others.

Major Ben Collier, one of the staff at Sandhurst, has a very honest take on the matter: 'Courage can ebb and flow. Some days you are up for the fight, other days you think: *It would be good if the enemy didn't engage us today.* Courage can also be infectious. In my patrol base, south of Helmand province, Afghanistan, there were nineteen of us. It was pretty intense. At one point, in Nad-e-Ali, we were in fire-fights with the Taliban three times a day, and that didn't let up for forty-six consecutive days. It was full-on without much let-up in between. Four hours' contact might be followed by half an hour's peace to grab something to eat. At times I really had to get a hold of myself; wake up, get a grip and be professional. The privilege to command equates to being responsible for everybody's lives, everybody's weapons, everybody getting home. You learn the art of understanding this responsibility at Sandhurst through the exercises you are put through as a Platoon Commander.'

THE BONDS OF TRUST

All the alumni featured in the previous chapter have one common denominator; they are all leaders who consider the welfare of their team before themselves, and that extends to helping strangers in trouble on a mountainside, or putting themselves at severe risk in the middle of a terrorist attack. It's about doing the right thing. Cadets are taught to ensure the needs of their troops are served before they think about their own; an officer will always eat last, and lead from the front. I think this kind of selflessness is at the core of what makes a fine officer, and I'm reminded of an operation during the First Gulf War, which illustrates the very essence of what it means to 'Serve to Lead':

As I mentioned earlier, in February 2003, the First Fusiliers Battle Group found itself on the western outskirts of the city of Basra overlooking the Shatt al-Arab waterway. Y Company was dug into a defensive position astride the main motorway into the city, about 2 km short of the main bridge across the waterway – 'Bridge 2' as it was known. The enemy held the far side of the river and we had reports that the bridge had been prepared for demolition. We'd been there for about forty-eight hours and our tanks had been involved in some action against enemy armour to the east. Our sister company, Z Company, was further south overlooking Bridge 4. Orders came down that we were to try and seize the bridges to ensure the routes into the city remained open. I planned the Y Company attack for first light the following morning.

The plan was to attack the enemy using armour up to the western bank, then dismount No 7 Platoon, who would advance on foot across the bridge to ensure demolitions were cleared. Trying to take armour across was not an option. Ollie Campbell, the Platoon Commander, was given a team of Engineers to help him clear the demolitions, should there be any. He led his soldiers out onto the bridge to begin looking for the demolitions, and about halfway across the enemy engaged them with small arms fire and mortars. Watching from the 'friendly' bank, I could see soldiers going down – one was literally blown off his feet. The attack stalled as our troops froze, pinned to the ground by enemy fire.

That was when I saw one man stand up, followed by a second. It was Ollie, the Platoon Commander, and his radio operator. As Ollie moved forward, more of his men stood and followed him. Through the fire, they inched slowly across the bridge, eventually reaching the far bank. In support, one of the tanks decided not to wait for the bridge to be cleared but followed to assist the lightly armed 7 Platoon. The bridge was cleared and successfully held.

For his actions that day, Ollie Campbell was awarded the Military Cross for gallantry. Many people have since asked him about what made him do what he did and, being the modest bloke he is, he always plays it down saying, 'I did what I was expected to do.' His actions demonstrate the very essence of army leadership – of what we teach at Sandhurst: the ability to overcome your own fear to inspire your people to do something every sinew in their body is telling them not to. Courage can be infectious. General Montgomery often talked about the hardest battle being the battle for the hearts of your men. That morning, Ollie was their example. They followed him not just because he was their officer, but because they believed in him. He had won his hardest battle long before he set foot on that bridge.

We are all faced with difficult situations – it might be a difficult change programme for the greater good of the company – and as leaders we sometimes have to tell people to do things they don't want to hear or do. When you find yourself in that position, you need to have already built those bonds of trust with your team. It's not an overnight process; it takes time and investment, demonstratin' genuinely care for them and that you will ensure they are loc' Only then will they stand and follow you. There is a reas' hurst motto is 'Serve to Lead'; servant leadership de' lead through the power of unselfish example, th' needs of your people before your own.

EMPOWERING OTHERS

Success comes from developing the people around you, coaching them individually towards their goals, encouraging their initiative, and empowering them to make their own decisions when the moment requires it. Whether it's in the army or in everyday life, it's always best to lead by good examples. It genuinely is about inspiring them. As General Dwight Eisenhower once said, 'You must know every single one of your [team]. It is not enough that you are the best soldier in that unit, that you are the strongest, the toughest, the most durable, and the best equipped technically. You must be their leader, their [parent], their mentor – even if you are half their age.'

When I was in First Fusiliers, my Commanding Officer used to know everything about everyone. He would come on a visit and stop by a sergeant and say, 'Sergeant Jones, how's Kimberley getting on after the new child? And how's the boy getting on?' I always wondered how he did it, because the effect it had was so considerable. The fact that he had taken the trouble to remember something about you went a very long way. I later found out his secret: he had ntastic driver, called Gromit. As they were driving to visit one of panies, Gromit would remind him, 'Don't forget to speak to es, he just had his second child, a son. His wife's called

Kimberley,' and so on and so forth for the other soldiers in the company. Admittedly, it was largely thanks to Gromit's incredible memory, but the Commanding Officer always made sure he was prepared because he more than understood that great teams are built on a bedrock of personal connections.

Serving to lead is helping others in your team be their best selves, while setting an example yourself by living your team's shared values. It's also about empowering your people, and sometimes that means being comfortable with the fact that at times members of your team are better equipped to lead than you. As a Platoon Commander, I was fortunate enough to be seconded to the Ulster Defence Regiment for a tour of duty in Northern Ireland during the Troubles. I spent six months commanding a platoon in Belfast. My soldiers were a fantastic bunch and I enjoyed every moment with them. The UDR no longer exists, but at that time it was made up of soldiers who came from the local community. Imagine, these were men and women who were conducting operations in and among a community in which they lived. They would come in and soldier during the day then return to their homes and families at night. This of course meant they had to remain covert – sometimes even their kids didn't know what they did. Brave men and women for whom I still have the greatest of respect.

One of the benefits of leading soldiers such as these was their local knowledge. They knew everyone and everything because they lived there. I couldn't possibly begin to know as much as they did and so I had to get used to them taking the lead when, in certain circumstances, they were better equipped and more knowledgeable than me.

In my four-man team in Belfast, the soldier who understood the answer to the specific issue was taking the lead because he was better informed. They were able to make the calls, while I still held the ultimate responsibility and accountability that came with my rank. Although I didn't realise it at the time, this is the essence of empowerment. Today's leaders can't possibly expect to know all the answers. As problems get more complex, we must become more comfortable with empowering others to take the lead. The concept of a leader and their followers is therefore outdated. If we are to truly unlock the potential of our people – and remember, the younger generations are better connected than any that has come before – then we, as leaders, need to be comfortable with letting them lead.

Farewell Address

It's been a pleasure writing this book, and sharing these nuggets of Sandhurst wisdom with you. I hope you'll find them useful and, as you move forward in your own life, remember to stand up straight and make your best nature, second nature. Keep setting new goals that challenge you, believe you can achieve them and, should you lose your way, don't be embarrassed or feel ashamed when you have to retrace your steps. Failure is a part of success. Try your best to keep a clear and uncluttered mind, sleep deeply, train hard and take care of yourself – inside and out. The autumn sun is spreading its last rays across the façade of Old College and turning the Corinthian columns a coppery gold as I bring our journey together to its end. I hope that you can take a kernel of this Sandhurst training and use it in your own life should you find yourself in a crisis, or looking for guidance to change your direction.

Major General Paul Nanson
Government House, October 2019

ACKNOWLEDGEMENTS

I would like to acknowledge all those who made this book possible, especially Richard Waters, Jess Ballance, Ben Brusey and the rest of the Penguin Random House team.

My greatest thanks go to those who contributed to the book by sharing their insights and vignettes. I would also like to pay tribute to the permanent staff – soldiers and civilians – whose dedication through the ages has provided us with the best example, and without whom Sandhurst would not be the amazing institution it is today.

Sandhurst has a special place in my heart, and in the heart of every British, and many international, army officers. I hope this book serves to reflect on the decades of history, heritage and ethos; and that the stories of Sandhurst training and experience, and the personal vignettes from field exercises and operations, will resonate with readers from all walks of life.

A Short Guide to 'Sandhurst Speak'

Attack phase – a phase of offensive combat directed against an enemy with the intent to kill, capture, or drive him from his position.

Aviation – military aircraft.

Babies' heads – these solid clumps of grass and earth can easily twist an ankle if you're not careful on your feet, and make for slow-going during Exercise Long Reach in the Brecon Beacons.

Battalion – a battalion is the smallest military unit capable of 'limited independent operations'.

Battle group – the basic building block of an army's fighting force. A battlegroup is formed around an infantry battalion or armoured regiment, and have attached 'specialist' arms such as Engineers or Artillery.

BATUS – stands for British Army Training Unit Suffield, a British Army unit located in Alberta, Canada. It is the British Army's largest armoured training facility and can accommodate large-scale exercises.

Bergen – the general British Armed Forces term for a large rucksack. We also have 'daysacks', which are smaller in size and, unsurprisingly, used for more short-term activities where less equipment is required.

Cadet or officer cadet – a rank held by military cadets during their training to become commissioned officers.

Civilian Street – normal civilian life.

Colour Sergeant – Colour Sergeants are Senior Non-Commissioned Officers and an important part of the instructor framework at the Royal Military Academy Sandhurst (RMAS), and they take the main burden of day-to-day training, especially during the first term.

Commanding Officer – the officer in command of a military unit. The Commanding Officer has ultimate authority over the unit, and is usually given wide latitude to run the unit as they see fit, within the bounds of military law.

Company – a military unit, typically consisting of 80–150 soldiers.

Condor Moment – when officers in the British Army take time to pause and reflect before going into action, a moment of 'courageous restraint'.

Drill – prepares soldiers through the practice and rehearsal of prescribed movements. Drill familiarises soldiers with the various battle formations and helps consolidate their knowledge of their weapons.

Field skills – basic techniques that are useful when in the field or on duty, such as camouflage and concealment, judging distance, individual movement techniques and group formations as well as how to cook army rations and find or create shelter.

FUP Green refers to Forming Up Place Green, which marked the beginning of the ground offensive stage of Operation Granby, more commonly known by its US title, Desert Storm, the operation to liberate Kuwait.

H-hour – the time at which an attack or advance begins.

Hot zone – an environment which represents an immediate threat to personnel from direct fire or from a known environmental threat.

LOE – stands for Limit Of Exploration, a set line on the map beyond which soldiers are ordered not to advance.

Log race – this race simulates the movement of an item of heavy weaponry/equipment, in this case a log, two miles across the battlefield. Points are awarded for determination, aggression and leadership.

MO – this stands for mission objective; the goal that you are setting out to achieve.

Objective Brass – a term used by the British Army to refer to a specific Iraqi artillery position during the First Gulf War.

OPFOR – abbreviation of 'opposing force', a military unit tasked with representing an enemy, usually for training purposes in war game scenarios.

Passing out – to graduate from the Sandhurst officer-training course.

Platoon – a military unit typically composed of two or more sections. An infantry platoon is typically the smallest military unit led by a commissioned officer, made up of between thirty and thirty-two people.

Regiment – the largest 'permanent' organisational unit, and because of their permanent nature, many regiments have long histories, often going back for centuries.

RMAS – Royal Military Academy Sandhurst.

Section – a military sub-subunit. A standard infantry section usually consists of between six and ten personnel. Two or more sections normally make up an army platoon.

Section attack – a practical exercise, based on technique and drills that teach the mechanics of a small unit assault and also help develop leadership and command training.

Serve to Lead – the motto of the Royal Military Academy Sandhurst. It is the concept of putting the needs of those you lead before your own, and a central concept of military leadership.

SOP – Standard Operating Procedures.

The Sovereign's Banner – used in the Trooping of the Colour during the Sovereign's Parade and awarded to the best platoon amongst the Division, known as the Sovereign's Platoon. The officer cadets in this platoon are selected on merit, from a competition in drill, orienteering, shooting and a cross-country race, ensuring they are of the best in endurance and teamwork.

The Sovereign's Parade – a parade held outside the Old College to mark the 'passing out' and the final parade at Sandhurst of the Senior Division. Three Sovereign's Parades are held each year as there are three different intakes of officer cadets each year.

Special Forces – a group of soldiers or Marines who are specially selected and tasked at the highest level. They operate in difficult and often challenging circumstances.

Stag, or 'to be on stag' – to be on guard duty, to stay awake and alert while others sleep.

The Sword of Honour – awarded to the British Army officer cadet considered by the Commandant to be, overall, the best from that intake.

TTP – Tactic Technique Procedures.

Waypoint – a stopping place on a journey, a point of reference that can be used for navigation, e.g. specific longitude and latitude of a location, or a well-known building or natural feature.